What People are Saying about American Psalms

"*American Psalms* challenges Christian patriots to put aside personal agendas, prejudices and partisanship, and pray for our leaders as God commands."

-Mike Huckabee, author of *A Simple Government*

"Joshua J. Masters' book, *American Psalms*, is tremendous! It is an uplifting, faith-filled treasury of inspiring prayers, solidly based in Scripture—'an answer to prayer' for our country at this critical time. With practical prayers for every area of life, including officeholders, farmers, business leaders, families, teachers, military, healthcare providers, Israel, Hollywood, and holidays, *American Psalms: Prayers for the Christian Patriot* is an easy to use and highly effective guide in spiritual intercession.

Joshua J. Masters calls us back to our nation's foundation of faith, just as Connecticut Governor Jonathan Trumbull did in his Proclamation of Fasting & Prayer, April 19, 1775, the day New England farmers 'fired the shot heard round the world' at Concord's old north bridge, that: 'God would graciously pour out His Holy Spirit on us to bring us to a thorough repentance and effectual reformation that our iniquities may not be our ruin; that He would restore, preserve and secure [our] liberties...and make the land a mountain of Holiness, and habitation of righteousness forever.'

I highly encourage every American to have Joshua J. Masters' book, *American Psalms: Prayers for the Christian Patriot*."

-William J. Federer, best selling author and nationally known speaker, author of *America's God and Country Encyclopedia of Quotations*

"*American Psalms* is a concise prayer guide for those who are new to intercession as well as those who are seasoned prayer leaders. In addition to motivating readers to pray for all aspects of our nation, this resource provides strategic prayer points and handy worksheets. This is a useful tool for all prayer leaders."

-Mary Bruce, National Day of Prayer Northeast National Area Leader

American Psalms
Prayers for the Christian Patriot

Joshua J. Masters

Follow us at www.AmericanPsalms.com

American Psalms: Prayers for the Christian Patriot
© 2012, 2016 Joshua J Masters
www.kingdomknight.com
www.AmericanPsalms.com

ISBN-13: 978-0-9857451-0-3
ISBN-10: 098574510X

Printed in the United States of America

May the prayers contained here be heard by our Lord, the sovereign King of all nations. May he bring peace, grace and prosperity to the United States.

"Bless the people of this land, be a Father to the fatherless, a Comforter to the comfortless, a Deliverer to the captives, and a Physician to the sick. Let Thy blessing be upon our friends, kindred and families. Be our Guide this day and forever through Jesus Christ in whose blessed form of prayer I conclude my weak petitions—Our Father, who art in heaven, hallowed be Thy name..."

-George Washington

Contents

x

Table of Inserts

The Praying Patriot

DiscipleTips

Acknowledgments

I am grateful to God for placing this book on my heart, and the changes he made in me as a result of writing it. I'm also grateful for the people he placed into my life who encouraged me through the process:

First, I must acknowledge my wife. She is the greatest answer to prayer in my life and the true intercessor in our household. Her encouragement and contribution to this process are invaluable. While it's true "I can do everything through Christ, who gives me strength" (Philippians 4:13 NLT), it probably wouldn't be organized without Gina.

A heartfelt thank you also to my parents, Patricia and Pastor Jay Dexter. My mom is a true prayer warrior in our lives, and my dad, a veteran himself, taught me how to be a Christian patriot from an early age. They have always been a source of great encouragement in my life.

Thanks also to Gina's parents, Ken and Madeleine Paquette. Their support is unyielding and I'm thankful for the part they play in our lives.

I'm also extremely grateful to Tamsin Laflam, who provided editing and proofreading services to this project. I value her friendship and talent.

Thank you to StaciAnne Grove who allowed me to photograph the memorial flag of her grandfather, First Lieutenant Frank E. Davis.

The photographs were used in the cover design in addition to several background images for inserts.

I'm also grateful to the many friends, accountability partners and small group members who encouraged me. Although it would be impossible to list them all, I'm particularly thankful to Mike James and Martha Balkin who've regularly let me bounce ideas off them, held me accountable and prayed with me over countless cups of coffee. Gina and I are also thankful for friends like Dan and Sue Ryan, Julie L. Wilder, Dan Martin, James and Linda Bushey, and our prayer partners, Jaime and Candice Allembert. They, along with others, have supported and strengthened us.

Lastly (and sincerely), I'm grateful for my dog, Franklin. He boosts my morale and his unconditional love is a welcome relief from the pressures of life. There were several occasions in which Franklin tried to contribute to this project by making unauthorized paw-strokes on the keyboard; he once typed an entire page when I stepped away. He fancies himself a writer like Snoopy, but unfortunately, none of his contributions made the final edit.

PART ONE

Preamble

Preamble

THE KINGDOM AND THE NATION

Every follower of Christ is called to be a citizen of God's Kingdom and an ambassador to their own nation. Any nation whose people turn toward God will then become a reflection of his will and mercy. One of America's greatest qualities is that, like the Kingdom of God, its citizenship is not based on race, ethnicity, birthright or fortune. For as America adopts those who come to her shores looking for liberty, the Lord adopts those who come into a relationship with him to receive true freedom. While one is a reflection, both bring hope to the hopeless and the promise of a better tomorrow.

The words engraved on the Statue of Liberty from the 1883 Emma Lazarus poem, "The New Colossus," welcoming those coming to America read:

> *"Give me your tired, your poor,*
> *Your huddled masses yearning to breathe free,*
> *The wretched refuse of your teeming shore.*
> *Send these, the homeless, tempest-tossed to me,*
> *I lift my lamp beside the golden door!"*

Is this not also the cry of our Father in Heaven? Those who are tired and poor, those who have never tasted liberty, those who have been tossed aside by society; they all come to America for what freedom can be offered by man, and to the Father for eternal freedom and grace. As Lady Liberty lifts her lamp so the lost can find their way, so did the Father lift up the Light of the World upon a cross so the lost might be found.

Our founders created an echo of God's Kingdom in America. However, an earthy institution that offers freedom can only be successful when the hand of the Almighty, the one who brings true freedom and liberty, is upon it. How can we expect to offer the gifts of God unless his hand is involved? Perhaps Benjamin Franklin said it best when he stood before the members of the Constitutional Convention and said:

> *God governs in the affairs of man. And if a sparrow cannot fall to the ground without his notice, is it probable that an empire can rise without his aid? We have been assured in the sacred writings that except the Lord build the house, they labor in vain that build it. I firmly believe this. I also believe that, without His concurring aid, we shall succeed in this political building no better than the builders of Babel.*

We, as Christian patriots, have a responsibility to lift our nation and our leaders up in prayer. This requires us to put aside our prejudice and political bias. Whether we call ourselves Republican or Democrat, progressive or moderate, conservative or liberal, we must remember that God has appointed those who are in power. Paul wrote, "Everyone must submit himself to the governing authorities, for there is no authority except that which God has established. The authorities that exist have been established by God" (Romans 13:1). That is not to say we can't disagree on policy, but it does mean we do so with respect and an examined heart. Whether or not we agree with our leaders, we're not only called to submit ourselves to those in authority, but are commanded to pray for them. Paul also wrote:

> *I urge, then, first of all, that requests, prayers, intercession and thanksgiving be made for everyone— for kings and all those in authority, that we may live peaceful and quiet lives in all godliness and holiness.* (1 Timothy 2:1-2)

The Book of Psalms is filled with the national prayers of Israel. In some, the Israelites praise the Father and in others they cry out in their suffering. But whatever the prayer, the psalms are filled with petitions of sincere emotion. We, as Christians in America, must stop keeping God at arm's length when we pray. We must kneel before him with sincerity and a heart for our nation.

Biblical history shows us that Israel prospered when it called out to God, but failed when it withdrew from a relationship with him. Can we expect more favor from God than Israel if we turn our attention away from him? Certainly not. God has made a clear promise to those who honor him:

> *If my people, who are called by my name, will humble themselves and pray and seek my face and turn from their wicked ways, then will I hear from heaven and will forgive their sin and will heal their land.* (2 Chronicles 7:14)

The purpose of this book is for American Christians to cry out to God with one voice, praying for his protection, grace, and guidance as we seek to become a reflection of his character. For he has promised to lift up that which is holy and heal that which is not.

We must again become a people who pray.
We must again become a nation who serves the Kingdom.

PRAYING THE WORD OF GOD

Each prayer in this book contains verses of scripture that serve as the basis for the prayer. They're also accompanied by an insert, entitled "In the Word." These inserts contain scripture references that support our coming before God with that particular request or praise.

If you want to increase the power of your prayers, grow closer in your walk with God or build your understanding of the Bible, there's nothing more effective than learning to pray directly from the Word of God. Christ is the very incarnation of God's Word. It is, in fact, one of his many names (John 1:14). Jesus is the source of our strength in prayer and the provision for our justified relationship with the Father. Jesus said, "I tell you the truth, my Father will give you whatever you ask *in my name*" (John 16:23). If Jesus *is* the Word, we should be praying with the authority found in scripture.

An important key to successfully praying scriptures is understanding why the Father gave us prayer in the first place. Remember, the purpose of prayer is to align us with God's will, not the other way around. John wrote, "This is the confidence we have in approaching God: that if we ask anything according to his will, he hears us" (1 John 5:14).

But how can we be sure we're praying for something in his will? God is always consistent and never changing. Timothy proved the reliability of the Bible in discerning God's will when he said:

> *All Scripture is God-breathed and is useful for teaching, rebuking, correcting and training in righteousness, so that the servant of God may be thoroughly equipped for every good work. (2 Timothy 3:16-17)*

When we base our prayers on the full Word of God, we know we're operating within his will.

A second reason to pray directly from scripture can be found in the character of the Father. We serve the only God who is revered for keeping his promises. In fact, Psalm 138:2 tells us the Father holds the integrity of his name and his Word above all things. As God said to Jeremiah, "You have seen correctly, for I am watching to see that my word is fulfilled" (Jeremiah 1:12). If we want to speak prayers of power, we need to be praying from scripture, because he has promised to fulfill his Word.

There's also an aspect of spiritual warfare involved in praying God's Word, because praying the scriptures defeats Satan. In fact, we should not only be praying from the scriptures, but we should also speak them out loud when we pray. The Enemy hates the Word of God because he knows it's the source of God's grace.

Satan constantly tries to twist the Word of God and take it out of context (e.g., Genesis 3:1-5), but when a true believer studies scripture, prays scripture and uses scripture within the context of God's complete message, Satan cannot defend against it. Praying God's Word is a weapon of righteousness:

> *For our struggle is not against flesh and blood, but against the rulers, against the authorities, against the powers of this dark world and against the spiritual forces of evil in the heavenly realms. (Ephesians 6:12)*

Using scripture-based prayer is our greatest hope of renewing the faith of America. It ensures that we come before the Father with a heart of worship and with a desire to see his will done in the United States.

HOW TO USE THIS BOOK

The pages that follow contain selected prayers for our nation. It is not meant to be, nor could it be, an exhaustive list of topics. Rather, it is meant to inspire believers to live the life of a Praying Patriot. You may certainly use the prayers contained in this book verbatim, but *my* prayer is that they will inspire you to come before the Lord as an intercessor for America who petitions God to bless the United States. The Psalms are primarily a book of praise. Israel pours out its heart in song with a continual sense of worship and reverence for the name of God. And while the prayers contained here are not specifically designed to be sung, we should approach all prayer with that same sense of worship and song in our hearts. This is how we should come to the Father when praying for America—with a heart of worship.

Dedicate yourself to praying for our country on a regular basis. Make a commitment before God to pray for our nation at least once a week for the next year, and encourage other believers to do the same. God does hear our prayers and they do make a difference.

There are fifty-two weekly prayers contained in this book (along with psalms for special days of prayer). I encourage you to read a prayer each week, but then come before God with what the Holy Spirit puts on your heart. When the Holy Spirit prompts you to pray, feel free to change the order of these prayers or pray something completely different. Pray for what God puts on your heart. There are several additional elements included in this book to help you grow in your spiritual formation and patriotic prayer life:

ELEMENTS OF THIS BOOK

In the Word
Each prayer contains an insert, entitled "In the Word." As discussed in a previous section, scripture-based prayer is the best way to ensure we're praying in the Father's will and coming before him with a sense of worship rather than selfishness. I encourage you to read the passages associated with each prayer and spend time in the Word when writing your own prayers.

The Praying Patriot

These inserts are designed to give you helpful hints in developing your own Patriot Prayers. They also include action items to help you make a difference in your community for the Kingdom. Remember, it's not enough to believe in Christ as our savior, we have to let him continually change our lives and allow him to use us in changing the lives of others.

Disciple Tips

Like "The Praying Patriot" inserts, these tips can be used to strengthen your prayer muscles as you pray for America, but they can also aid in general spiritual formation. We must continually grow in Christ, allowing him to sanctify us as we mature in our walk with him.

Patriot Quotes

Many prominent Americans have spoken about God's role in the blessings of our country. These quotes are meant to inspire modern believers to see the incredible influence God has had on our leaders and in the prosperity of America.

The Praying Patriot Worksheets

The back of the book contains worksheets that will help you remember whom to pray for. Although the prayers contained in this book do not include names, your prayers will be more powerful when you use the actual names of our leaders. Use the worksheets in the back of this book to create a prayer list for yourself. Post them on your refrigerator or on your desk at work.

PART TWO

Weekly Prayers
for the Nation

WEEK ONE:
A Declaration of Prayer

F ather God, you are the King of kings and
the Lord of lords.[1] Your kingdom is
sovereign above all others; yours is the
Kingdom of Glory, which will reign in
righteousness for eternity. I pray our nation
would be a light to the world, that it might see
your kingdom in us.

In The Word

[1] *I Timothy 6:15*

[2] *I Timothy 2:1-3*

[3] *Romans 13:1*

[4] *John 16:8-11*

You have commanded us to pray for those who
are in authority,[2] because there is no
government that you have not appointed.[3] I am
grateful I've been given the opportunity to
share in the liberty and freedom you have
bestowed upon the United States.

I confess that our nation can be prideful; our
pride should be in your abilities, not our own.
We cannot succeed without your grace and
blessing. For you have said:

> *If my people, who are called by my name,*
> *will humble themselves and pray and seek*
> *my face and turn from their wicked ways,*
> *then will I hear from heaven and will*
> *forgive their sin and will heal their land.*
> *(2 Chronicles 7:14)*

I will call upon your name; I will humble myself

before you for the sake of my walk with Christ, and for the sake of my country.

I will call upon your name for the sake of our leaders, for the sake of our citizens and for the sake of our future. I ask that you would hear my prayers and restore our nation. Send the Holy Spirit to convict us of our sin[4] and call other believers to join in prayer for America. I pray you will hear our cries from heaven and fulfill your promise to heal our land.

Because you have commanded me to pray and because I have a heart for this nation, I commit myself to this course of action: I will lift up the United States and her leaders to you in prayer. I will remember that it is you alone who grants liberty and freedom. I will put aside my own bias and political views so that I may pray for our leaders to become more like you, instead of judging them for not being more like me.

I thank you for this great country you have allowed me to be a part of. May your light be seen from the shores of America throughout the world.
    AMEN.

WEEK TWO:

A Prayer for our President

G iver of godly wisdom,[1] you have called me to pray for all men and for those who have authority over me.[2] There is no greater authority in our land than the president of the United States, and I will commit to praying for the office and administration of my president.

We have elected people to the presidency I've voted for and others whom I have not. Yet it is you who has anointed the president,[3] and I will pray for your purpose to be fulfilled in the president's life. Give me a heart of compassion for the president and allow me to be an unbiased intercessor for this administration.

I know the one you've called to be president is faced with adversities I will never know. There are daily decisions of life and death making their way to the president's desk. These decisions affect the lives of millions of your children (and those who have not yet found solace in your grace). In these moments, I ask that you would send the Holy Spirit to our president with the gift of wisdom.[4]

Each president has their own experience—experience given to them by you. True wisdom,

In The Word

[1] *Proverbs 2:6*

[2] *I Timothy 2:1-3*

[3] *Romans 13:1*

[4] *I Corinthians 12:8*

[5] *Revelation 1:8*

though, comes only from the one who can see the end of things as easily as their beginning: the Alpha and Omega.[5]

No leader would confess a lack of wisdom to their people, but I pray the Holy Spirit would convict the president's heart to seek your wisdom above his own. For you have promised to give wisdom in times of trial to those who ask:

> *If any of you lacks wisdom, he should ask God, who gives generously to all without finding fault, and it will be given to him. (James 1:5)*

We have seen through the history of Israel in scripture that the success of a nation greatly relies on how its leader reveres your sovereignty. I pray for our president, that he would seek you in all things. Give our president the wisdom, knowledge and protection that can only be granted by the Almighty God of our nation.
  AMEN.

The Praying Patriot

PRESIDENTIAL PRAYERS

When praying for the president, use his or her name. You're not only praying for the office, but for the individual. Remember to pray for their family as well. Often the political attacks on the president affect the presidential family more than the office itself.

WAYS TO PRAY FOR OUR PRESIDENT:

- When the president is about to give a speech or interview
- When the president is hosting a visiting dignitary
- When the president is on foreign soil
- When a natural disaster has befallen America
- When the president or his family is under scrutiny
- Daily when we are at war

WEEK THREE:

A Prayer for the Legislature

G od of our nation, you are both the giver of the Law[1] and our deliverer from the effects of the Law.[2] You are a god of justice and righteousness. Lift up those who are crafting the laws of America, for you have called us to obey those who are in authority over us. Your servant Peter wrote:

In The Word

[1] *Exodus 20:1-21*

[2] *Romans 7:1-6*

[3] *I Peter 2:11-25*

[4] *Exodus 7:13*

[5] *Isaiah 9:6*

> *Submit yourselves for the Lord's sake to*
> *every authority instituted among men:*
> *whether to the king, as the supreme*
> *authority, or to governors, who are sent by*
> *him to punish those who do wrong and to*
> *commend those who do right.*
> *(1 Peter 2:13-14)*

You have called us to serve the laws of man, that in doing so we might serve your kingdom.[3] This puts a burden on those serving as legislators to write laws of justice and liberty.

Protect our senators and congressmen from the dangers of partisanship for the sake of partisanship. Instead, send the Holy Spirit to give them a heart for doing your will. Give them the courage to fight for what you've called them to do, and the humility to accept your will when it is aligned with those they don't agree with.

Above all, do not allow their hearts to be hardened like Pharaoh's,[4] such that they might lose their ability to see your glory. I pray our lawmakers would keep the spirit of the law in their hearts as they craft legislation. Do not allow them to neglect the true purpose of the law, which is to promote liberty and benefit America's citizens. Do not let them be misled like the Pharisees, of whom the Lord said:

> *Woe to you, teachers of the law and Pharisees, you hypocrites! You give a tenth of your spices—mint, dill and cumin. But you have neglected the more important matters of the law—justice, mercy and faithfulness. You should have practiced the latter, without neglecting the former. (Matthew 23:23)*

Give our legislators your heart for justice, mercy and faithfulness. Give them the peace that can only come from the Holy Spirit and a relationship with the Prince of Peace.[5] Protect our senators and congressmen; encourage and strengthen them so they might serve the American people with integrity and a desire for you.
   AMEN.

The Praying Patriot

ENCOURAGING LEGISLATORS

Most congressmen and senators only hear from their constituency when they're upset about something. People often complain that those in congress don't represent the people—that they're only there for the sake of their own power.

Have you ever been in a job where you feel overworked and completely unappreciated? A little encouragement goes a long way in preventing someone from becoming bitter or hardened. Our senators and congressmen have gone to Washington to serve us, but what have we done to serve them?

Call your representatives and encourage them. Tell them that you appreciate them. Take the time to research the legislation they're working on and let them know that you're praying for their work.

WEEK FOUR:
A Prayer for the Judicial System

J udge of the living and of the dead,[1] You are fair and righteous. You love justice and hate iniquity.[2] As the greatest of judges and creator of mercy, I pray you would have your hand upon the judges of America's courts.

In The Word

[1] Acts 10:42

[2] Isaiah 61:8

[3] Psalm 106:3

Lift up those who serve in the judicial branch of our government and allow them to preside with fairness and mercy:

> "This is what the LORD Almighty says: 'Administer true justice; show mercy and compassion to one another.'" (Zechariah 7:9)

I pray also for the salvation of our judges. May they, who hold the lives of many in their hands, be convicted by the Holy Spirit to repent of their sin. Only one who walks in the righteousness of Jesus can truly administer godly justice. For you have said:

> Evil people don't understand justice, but those who follow the LORD understand completely. (Proverbs 28:5, NLT)

You have promised to bless those who maintain justice and constantly do right;[3] as our judges follow you in administering justice within their own lives and for the American people, I ask that you would bestow your blessings on them.

Give them the ability to separate their political beliefs from their duty to the law, their country and the God of Justice. Allow them to raise the banner of your will while proclaiming the American ideal of "liberty and justice for all."

    AMEN.

WEEK FIVE:
Prayer for America's Sovereignty

S overeign Lord, your kingdom rules over all[1] and no one can claim authority over your kingship. You have created the heavens and the earth; you have made mankind to rule over every living creature,[2] but you alone will sit upon the throne of David forever![3]

I pray our nation would submit to no authority other than that of Jesus Christ, and while we seek good relations with our neighbors, do not allow the seduction of globalization to strip us of our independence. May our identity be in you, not in the world.

But in our sovereignty, allow us to share our blessings with those in need, for your kingdom is generous. Let us show mercy, for your kingdom is merciful. Let us sacrifice for those who are not free, for the sacrifice of your kingdom has set us free.

Millions have died that we might have independence and authority over this land— that our sovereignty might give our people hope, liberty and freedom. May our nation be blessed as we imitate the glory of your kingdom.
AMEN.

In The Word

[1] *Psalm 103:19*

[2] *Genesis 1:28-29*

[3] *Luke 1:32*

"*I have been driven many times upon my knees by the overwhelming conviction that I had nowhere else to go. My own wisdom, and that of all about me, seemed insufficient for that day.*"

-*Abraham Lincoln*

PATRIOT QUOTE

WEEK SIX:

A Prayer for our Military Leaders

ehovah-Sabaoth,[1] Lord and commander of the heavenly armies, it was under your authority that Samson overcame a thousand men with the jawbone of a donkey,[2] and under your command David slew a giant with a single stone.[3] You stood before Joshua, sword drawn, and led him to victory over Jericho.[4] And you command Michael and his army of angels, who cast out the poison of Lucifer's pride from Heaven.[5] You are the giver of victory in combat.

I pray that our military leaders would seek your wisdom in battle; that they would seek integrity and righteousness in every order they give.

May they see that those submitting to your commands understand authority and have greater success commanding their own troops. For when Christ offered to go to the Roman Centurion's home and heal his servant, the soldier recognized the true authority of your command, saying:

> *"Lord, I do not deserve to have you come under my roof. But just say the word, and my servant will be healed. For I myself am a man under authority, with soldiers under*

In The Word

[1] *I Samuel 17:45*

[2] *Judges 15:14-19*

[3] *I Samuel 17*

[4] *Joshua 5:13-6:27*

[5] *Revelation 12:7-9*

[6] *Romans 12:6-8*

[7] *I Corinthians 12:8*

me. I tell this one, 'Go,' and he goes; and that one, 'Come,' and he comes. I say to my servant, 'Do this,' and he does it."
(Matthew 8:8-9)

You have only to speak and we find victory over armies and healing for our servants. Give our military leaders a humble heart to recognize your command just as the Roman Centurion did.

Send the Holy Spirit to comfort them, for the lives of many soldiers are in their hands. Bless them with the gifts of leadership[6] and wisdom,[7] so their campaigns will succeed and their troops will be safe.

Those you call to evangelism represent Christ in the way they live, not the words they speak. May our commanding officers be reminded that this is also true of our military. They, and the men and women who serve under them, are the true ambassadors of America. They bring the light of freedom to those who live in darkness—not in concept, but in the way they interact with the civilians they come in contact with.

Father, protect those who have been charged with overseeing the troops who have been sent to protect me. I am grateful for their sacrifice, and pray for their success in all things.
AMEN.

WEEK SEVEN:

A Prayer for our Troops

rotector of nations, you are our strength and our shield.[1] I give you all the glory and praise for the blessings you have bestowed on our country.

In The Word

[1] *Psalm 28:7*

[2] *Mark 10:45*

[3] *Matthew 28:20*

I ask you to bless and protect our soldiers. They sacrifice more than most of us know in protection of the freedom and liberty you have given us. These are the men and women who truly have a servant's heart;[2] they are the Americans who truly understand living a sacrificial life for others. Place your angels of protection before them and give them a sense of your hand upon them.

Our troops have left their families and the comfort of their homes to ensure liberty for the United States and freedom for those who are oppressed. Do not allow them to feel isolated or alone in their deployment. Instead, let them hear your promise to be with them always[3] and find peace in your strength.

In moments of fear, let them find comfort from the Holy Spirit. Give them courage as you did David when he wrote:

The LORD is my light and my salvation—
so why should I be afraid?
The LORD is my fortress, protecting me from danger,
so why should I tremble?
When evil people come to devour me,
when my enemies and foes attack me,
they will stumble and fall.
Though a mighty army surrounds me,
my heart will not be afraid.
Even if I am attacked,
I will remain confident.
(Psalm 27:1-3, NLT)

Give our soldiers a knowledge of your Word, and allow them to feel our prayers of protection upon them. Speak to their hearts a promise of protection for their families so they might be fully focused on the job before them.

Our soldiers will no doubt walk through fire and see terrible things as they are deployed. I pray that they would seek you in the darkest moments of their mission and see your hand in the beauty of creation that surrounds them. Let them see your hope where there seems only to be hopelessness, your mercy in lands that are being oppressed and your peace where there seems only to be war.

Whether stationed overseas or at a base on native soil, whether deployed to the front line or doing administrative tasks, whether a seasoned warrior or a soldier training for their first mission, whether a retired veteran or a recruit just leaving home, bless those who serve our nation. May they find respect and support from those of us who benefit from their sacrifice.

    AMEN.

WEEK EIGHT:

A Prayer for Military Families

A dvocate and Comforter,[1] you see the suffering our world does not acknowledge. You see the sacrifice of those who do so in silence. You yourself felt such sacrifice that your heart and lips cried out, "My God, My God, why have you forsaken me?"[2]

I confess I don't always see the quiet sacrifice of those who are left behind by our soldiers. Is their sacrifice any less? Do they not live with fear and uncertainty so I might have security and safety? Are they not separated from their family so I might be with mine? Though I may not see their sacrifice and pain, you are the Comforter who sees every tear:

> *You keep track of all my sorrows.*
> *You have collected all my tears in your*
> *bottle. You have recorded each one in your*
> *book. (Psalm 56:8, NLT)*

I pray Lord, that you would see the tears of our military families—that you would put your arms of protection around them.

To those who are longing to hear from their loved ones, send them word. To those who have

In The Word

[1] **John 14:26**

[2] **Matthew 27:46**

[3] **I John 3:1**

[4] **Psalm 37:7**

had family lay down their lives for our country, send the Holy Spirit to comfort them.

Father, you have made us your children.³ You have suffered with those who've lost their loved ones; you have shared tears with families who are separated, for they are your children. And just as you felt the pain of being separated from the Son, just as you watched him die to save others, so do our military families suffer.

Protect their soldiers and lift up their spirits. Strengthen their resolve and encourage their hearts. I ask that you would see their needs and provide for them. Give me and my community a heart of compassion toward these families because they have served with a heart of humility and sacrifice.

Bring great blessings upon their households, their children and their finances. See their offering and let them rest in you.⁴
    AMEN.

The Praying Patriot

Praying for the Military

Many churches have a team devoted to praying for the soldiers from the community and their families. Get involved in praying for those troops and provide for the needs of their families. If a group doesn't already exist at your church, ask your pastor if you can start one. Here are a few other ideas:

- Contact the commanding officer or chaplain for your state's National Guard base. Ask how you can be praying for the troops in your area.
- Adopt a soldier with your small group and commit to praying for him or her. You can even send care packages to both the soldier and their family.
- Visit a local VA hospital and pray with the soldiers who are being treated.
- Whenever you see a bumper sticker or specialized license plate indicating military service, pray for that soldier and their family. You may not know who they are or what their story is, but God does.

WEEK NINE:

A Call to Repentance

L ord Our Righteousness,[1] you alone are holy, and you have seen the sins of our nation. Have we squandered the blessings you've given us like the prodigal son who wasted his inheritance on selfish gain?[2] How far have we strayed from the country you've called us to be?

In The Word

[1] *Jeremiah 23:6*

[2] *Luke 15:11-16*

[3] *John 16:8*

[4] *Luke 15:17-32*

But can a nation sin? We cannot hide behind the banner of our nation, for a country is only unrighteous through the sins of those who are in the land. When we fall to temptation, it is reflected in our country; we are responsible for our actions. The Holy Spirit wrote through James:

> but each person is tempted when they are dragged away by their own evil desire and enticed. Then, after desire has conceived, it gives birth to sin; and sin, when it is full-grown, gives birth to death. (James 1:14-15)

The sins of the nation are the sins of the people, born of our own evil desires. I pray you would send the Holy Spirit to show us where we have faltered as a people and convict us of our sin.[3] Give us a heart of repentance. Allow us to turn our hearts toward the Father with a changed heart, just as the prodigal son returned with a renewed faith in his father's grace and provision.[4]

Forgive me for not representing you in all things I do. I know my actions affect my community and the country. Reveal to me where I have failed and allow me the strength to renounce those sins. I pray this for myself and my countrymen. It is not enough to say we believe in the Lord; we must show it as we interact with the world. We must not profess the truth without living it. We must desire to be sanctified and made more like you. For you have written:

> *But if anyone obeys his word, God's love is truly made complete in him. This is how we know we are in him: Whoever claims to live in him must walk as Jesus did. (1 John 2:5-6)*

Allow the world to see your mercy through our actions; allow others to see Christ in the way we live our lives. Give us a desire to turn toward you and seek your righteousness as we strive to obey your Word. Sanctify us as a nation and allow us to be a light to the world for your purpose.
AMEN.

WEEK TEN:

A Prayer for America's Faith

F aithful and True[1] God, having confessed our unrighteousness, I ask you to heal our nation and sanctify us as a people. Allow us to grow in our faith so we might represent the heart of our Father. Help us to remember that the sovereignty of our nation lies within the Kingdom of God. May our country walk in a way that reflects your light to every nation, and may we praise you with great faithfulness.

> *Great is the LORD and most worthy of praise; his greatness no one can fathom. (Psalm 145:3)*

We have called ourselves a Christian nation; we have claimed to be Christian for the sake of labels and polls. But do not allow us to wear the title of Christian without giving us a heart for your sanctification. Do not give us peace with a simple belief in Christ. Instead, let us become followers of Christ.

Let us not take pride in having Christ at our table for show like Simon the Pharisee—he sought to use Jesus for his own agenda. Instead, give us a heart like the sinful woman who wept at your feet for the opportunity to serve you.[2]

This is my prayer: that we would not be lukewarm[3] Christians, that we would not use your name when it is convenient while rejecting the life you have called us to live. Give us a desire to grow in our faith.

The Enemy follows your blessings with a temptation of pride. He whispers into America's ears that our strength comes from our own power, and that we've earned our wealth through our own works. Let us be forever reminded that you are the giver of freedom and liberty. You are the source of all blessings. Let us embrace the words of Peter, who wrote:

> *For you know that it was not with perishable things such as silver or gold that you were redeemed from the empty way of life handed down to you from your ancestors, but with the precious blood of Christ, a lamb without blemish or defect. He was chosen before the creation of the world, but was revealed in these last times for your sake. Through him you believe in God, who raised him from the dead and glorified him, and so your faith and hope are in God. (I Peter 1:18-21)*

I thank you for the sacrifices our ancestors made in your name to bring freedom to this land, but ask that we might remain focused on your strength, your wisdom and your heart. Show us the path that leads to a closer walk with you. Allow us to seek after you as the lamp before our feet and the light for America's path.[4]
    AMEN.

WEEK ELEVEN:

A Prayer for America's Generosity

C reator of all things,[1] the world belongs to you alone. Everything and everyone upon the earth is yours.[2]

We are stewards of America's wealth, but it is not ours to do with as we please. Everything we have belongs to you. For as you said to Israel through your prophet, the silver and gold of our land is yours.[3] Help us to remember your title in our giving. For you have declared:

In The Word

[1] *Genesis 1:1*

[2] *Psalm 24:1*

[3] *Haggai 2:8*

[4] *Romans 12:5*

[5] *John 3:16*

> *Those who give to the poor will lack nothing, but those who close their eyes to them receive many curses. (Proverbs 28:27)*

I thank you for America's generous character. You have broken our hearts for those in need. When Haiti was devastated by earthquakes, you turned America's heart toward their recovery. When New Orleans was all but destroyed by floods, you spoke into our souls so the needs of the displaced might be met. Your Holy Spirit was the source of our compassion toward Indonesia and Japan when they lost so many loved ones to the Tsunamis.

As a nation, we reach out to the oppressed and the diseased. You have given us the resources to reach your healing hand out to every corner of the globe. Allow us to continue this generosity, but let us do so as individuals in your name.

So many of us have been blessed beyond the comprehension of other nations. Even those of us who struggle are rich compared to so many in other countries. Do not let us take that for granted any longer. Instead, let us see the sick and impoverished through your eyes of mercy. If we are the body of Christ,[4] let us reach out your hands to those in need; let us be your feet when going into the world; let us have your heart for the lost and oppressed.

As we give, I pray we would give sacrificially. You have such love for us that you sacrificed your only son,[5] and I ask you to give us that same heart of sacrifice for those who are lost. Let us see our giving as an act of worship. For when you return you will see our generosity as a pleasing sacrifice to our God:

> *"The King will reply, 'Truly I tell you, whatever you did for one of the least of these brothers and sisters of mine, you did for me.'"*
> *(Matthew 25:40)*

May our hearts and minds be turned toward you in our giving, and may we continue to be ambassadors of your grace both at home and abroad. Bless us that we might bless others in your name.
  AMEN.

WEEK TWELVE:
A Prayer for America's Freedom

Blessed Hope[1] of Our Salvation, you are the very foundation of freedom. You are the source of liberty and your name is the hope of all nations.[2]

You have blessed America with unparalleled liberties and I ask that our focus would be upon your grace. Do not let us surrender our freedoms in the name of conformity, and do not allow our hearts to be hardened toward our freedom in Christ.

May we not be like the Israelites who longed for slavery in Egypt rather than following the difficult path to freedom.[3] Do not allow us to be like those early Christians who sought to abandon your gift of liberty and return to the chains of legalism.[4] For you intend your children to be free:

> *It is for freedom that Christ has set us free. Stand firm, then, and do not let yourselves be burdened again by a yoke of slavery. (Galatians 5:1)*

I am so grateful to those who've sacrificed their lives and their loved ones for the freedoms we share in this country.

In The Word

[1] *Titus 2:13*

[2] *Matthew 12:21*

[3] *Numbers 14:1-4*

[4] *Hebrews 3*

[5] *Ephesians 3:12*

I ask you to bless their families and comfort the broken-hearted. Those who serve now or have served in the past have been separated from their families and have sacrificed their lives to defend the freedom you have afforded us.

Never allow me to forget the great price that has been paid for my freedom. Our soldiers and their families have suffered a sacrifice I cannot comprehend. Christians have been tortured and killed for my right to worship you without fear of persecution. And the greatest sacrifice of all was giving your only son to be ridiculed and killed so that I might stand before you with confidence and freedom.[5]

Protect the freedom of this great land and do not allow us to take for granted what you have given us. Above all, do not let us forget that true freedom and liberty never comes from a nation, but from you alone.

 AMEN.

WEEK THIRTEEN:
A Prayer for our Local Leaders

B lessed and only Almighty God,[1] your Word is the great authority in our lives. Send your Holy Spirit into my life and into the lives of those in my community, that we might see your truth.

I lift up those who are in authority over me. Not just for the president and congress, but for those serving my community at the local level. You have placed them in positions of power[2] and I pray they would seek integrity and righteousness in their post:

> *When the godly are in authority, the people rejoice. But when the wicked are in power, they groan. (Proverbs 29:2, NLT)*

I pray first for the authorities in my home town. Give those on the city council and our mayor the wisdom to balance the overall good of our town with the individual liberties of our citizens.

I lift up our local representatives who travel to the statehouse and act on behalf of our community. May they be moved to seek your wisdom in their votes, for you have promised to give wisdom to those who ask.[3]

In The Word

[1] I Timothy 6:15

[2] Romans 13:1

[3] James 1:5

39

I also give thanks and pray for our senators and representatives in Washington. Protect them as they travel from our state, and let them remember us in their politics. Many of them give up a great deal of time with their families to serve us in the nation's capitol and I ask you to bless their families for that sacrifice.

May our governor seek your face in all things. Whether dealing with the state legislature or representing our state outside its borders, I pray our governor would be a person of great faith and that she might find you in times of trouble.

I also give thanks for those serving in command of our local National Guard troops, who have authority over the sons and daughters of our community. Bless our troops and their families. They are our neighbors and our loved ones, our husbands and our wives... but they are also the protectors of our sovereignty as a state and a country.

Change my heart and my attitude toward our local leadership. Give me the same passion to pray for them as they have to serve me, regardless of their political affiliation. Allow our community to serve those who serve us, and do not let us be blinded by political anger:

Mockers stir up a city, but the wise turn away anger.
(Proverbs 29:8)

AMEN.

WEEK FOURTEEN:
A Prayer for our Firefighters

P rotector from the flames, you have written down my name and saved me from eternal fire.[1] Your grace is sufficient for me,[2] and I praise you for the protection and salvation you bring.

Today, I lift up those who walk into the heat of blazing fires to save others. I pray for the protection of those men and women who daily risk their lives to save those they've never met.

You are a god who walks into the fiery furnace to deliver your children, and just as you appeared in the flames with Shadrach, Meshach and Abednego,[3] I ask you to be with our firemen as they walk willingly into the fire. May they emerge from the danger unharmed, as when you saved Daniel's friends from the fire:

> *They saw that the fire had not harmed their bodies, nor was a hair of their heads singed; their robes were not scorched, and there was no smell of fire on them. (Daniel 3:27b)*

And when those who save are saved by you, may you receive the praise and glory.

Give them steadiness of feet that they might

In The Word

[1] *Revelation 20:15*

[2] *2 Corinthians 12:9*

[3] *Daniel 3:26*

[4] *Psalm 119:105*

navigate through the darkness with your Word as a lamp before their feet.[4]

Give them the ears to hear the call of those trapped behind the obscurity of smoke and the roar of fire's voice.

Give them clear vision that they might see those who cannot call out for help.

Give them courage in the face of danger and the wisdom needed to protect themselves and save others. Above all, may your grace and compassion be reflected in their lives both in and out of the flame.

I thank you for their sacrifice and the sacrifice of their families. They have seen an earthly reflection of the eternal horror, and I pray it would move them to seek you.
   AMEN.

WEEK FIFTEEN:

A Prayer for our Police Officers

F ather of Heaven and Earth, you sent your son to be a servant and bring justice to the nations.[1] You have brought us peace and protection through his sacrifice, and I praise you for the eternal protection you bring those who look upon you with faith.

In The Word

[1] *Isaiah 42:1*

[2] *I Cor. 10:24*

[3] *Ephesians 6:16*

[4] *Philippians 4:7*

The police officers of my community have dedicated their lives to the protection and service of others. They have embraced your command to put the good of others above their own.[2] Bless them for the protection they bring to us, even when we don't see their sacrifice.

You are a god who honors service to others, for you yourself left the glory of Heaven to serve those who did not know you, and commanded us to serve with that same passion, saying:

> *Your attitude should be the same as that of Christ Jesus: Who, being in very nature God, did not consider equality with God something to be grasped, but made himself nothing, taking the very nature of a servant, being made in human likeness.*
> *(Philippians 2:5-7)*

Having answered that call, I ask you to protect our police force even as they put their lives in danger to protect me and my family from harm.

When they feel unappreciated and segregated from the ones they serve, send the Holy Spirit to comfort and encourage them. For you know the heartache of being rejected by the ones you came to save.

When they face danger, give them wisdom and a sense of calm. Though they wear a shield as a symbol of their service, give them the protection that only comes from a shield of faith.[3]

Remember also the children and spouses of our officers—they too have sacrificed for our community and face worrisome nights so that I might rest peacefully. Bring them the peace that passes all understanding,[4] and bless them for having the heart of a servant.

I thank you for the service of our police officers and pray you would remind me to thank them in my words and actions toward them.
  AMEN.

WEEK SIXTEEN:
A Prayer for our Teachers

R abboni,[1] you reveal truth through your Holy
Spirit[2] and teach us of your grace and
mercy. You have called us your children,[3]
and teach us the ways of righteousness,
knowledge and wisdom so we might become
mature in our walk.

The teachers of our children have been given
this same charge. They too are called to bring
righteousness, knowledge and wisdom into
maturity within our youngest generations.
Their godly work will not be in vain, for you
have promised:

> Train a child in the way he should go,
> and when he is old he will not turn from it.
> (Proverbs 22:6)

I pray a great blessing on our teachers, and ask
that they might seek your wisdom in teaching
our children. Send the Holy Spirit to reveal
your truth to them, so they might in turn share
that truth with their students, both in what they
say and in the way they conduct their lives.

Above all, give our teachers the courage to train
our children to seek truth on their own, without
bias or prejudice, because you have promised

In The Word

[1] *John 20:16*

[2] *John 16:13*

[3] *I John 3:1*

[4] *Matthew 7:7*

[5] *Romans 12:6-8*

45

that those who seek truth will find it.[4] Your truth reveals itself to those whose eyes are open.

May our teachers be recognized for their passion and when they are not recognized, may they know you see their service and remember them. You have given them the spiritual gifts of teaching, leadership, encouragement and service.[5] Allow them to use those gifts with wisdom, responsibility and an eye toward your purpose.

I thank you for our teachers and ask for a revival of faith in our schools. You are ever present in our lives, as the teacher of your children. Praise be to our teacher and savior, who came to us with compassion so we might learn of your grace, forgiveness and wisdom.
   AMEN.

The Praying Patriot

PRAYING FOR TEACHERS

Teachers often find themselves under attack for the smallest of reasons, with little encouragement. Make an effort to thank your child's teacher for their work and pray for them regularly. Remember, your child's teacher spends a great deal of time with them and you want them to succeed.

WAYS TO PRAY FOR YOUR CHILD'S TEACHERS:

- Pray for teachers *with* your child and teach your child to respect teachers.
- Pray for the teacher's lesson plans and creativity.
- Ask God to show you ways to encourage your child's teacher.
- Pray for teachers during field trips.
- Even if you don't know anything about the teacher's personal life, pray for their happiness, peace and protection outside the classroom. Also, pray for their families and personal relationships.

WEEK SEVENTEEN:
A Call to Prayer and Fasting

H oly One[1] and God Most High,[2] I confess that I've allowed bitterness and apathy to corrupt my heart. I have allowed partisanship to taint my prayers in seeking your grace for America. Sanctify my mind and give me a heart of forgiveness as I stand in prayer[3] for our nation.

In The Word

[1] **Acts 2:27**

[2] **Genesis 14:20**

[3] **Mark 11:25**

[4] **Romans 8:1**

[5] **Matthew 9:15**

[6] **Joel 2:15**

I ask you to give our Christian patriots a passion for America's future in your will. Have the Holy Spirit convict us of our sin, destroying the enemy's arrows of apathy and hate. Let them instead give way to prayer and fasting for our country. As the day of your return draws ever closer, you have said:

> *"Even now... return to me with all your heart, with fasting and weeping and mourning."*
> *(Joel 2:12)*

How long has it been since we sought your peace with a truthful heart? How long since we wept in prayer and fasting before you?

Have we abused the freedom your grace gives us from the law?[4] Have we neglected America's freedom of worship by ignoring worship?

47

I pray for our hearts to change and for there to be a revival of prayer and fasting in the American church. For you said we would pray and fast until your return,[5] and we want to be drawn closer to you.

Just as the trumpets were blown to declare a time of fasting in Jerusalem,[6] I pray American Christians would hear your call and be drawn closer to you through prayer, fasting and the reading of your Word. Change my heart and reveal your will to me and my fellow Christians across this land.

AMEN.

— Disciple Tip

FASTING CHALLENGE

Did you know Abraham Lincoln declared a national day of fasting in order to heal the nation? Spending time fasting and in prayer is one of the most powerful tools we have in drawing closer to God, discerning his will and fulfilling his purpose for our lives. Whether seeking God in times of mourning, overcoming sin or embarking on a new stage of life, the Father will use your sacrifice to renew and strengthen you.

Fasting is not to be taken lightly. Be sure you research safe methods of fasting before you begin. There are many excellent Christian books on fasting, and you should consult a doctor if you have health concerns.

THINGS TO KEEP IN MIND:

- There are different types of fasting. While some people consume only water during a fast, others, like Daniel, deny themselves anything but vegetables (Daniel 1:8-17). Again, research fasting methods before you begin.
- Remember, the purpose of fasting is to draw closer to God. Spend extra time in prayer and in reading the Bible. Limit your media intake and worldly activities during the fast.
- Start slow. Regular fasting can become a disciplined part of life, but like anything else, you have to build that discipline. You don't decide to become a runner on Monday and do a marathon on Tuesday. God will honor your sacrifice even if you start with one meal.
- Fast with a spouse, small group or friend. This will increase accountability and give you someone to pray with. But aside from your doctor and those you're fasting with, keep your fast a secret. Fasting is about your relationship with God, not showing others how disciplined you are (Matthew 6:16-18).

WEEK EIGHTEEN:

A Prayer for America's Pastors

G reat Shepherd and overseer of our souls,[1] I lift up our American pastors to you, the Chief Shepherd.[2] May you protect their hearts, bodies, souls and minds that they may resist the temptation of the enemy, who surely wants them to fail. You have called our clergy to be a beacon of sanctification to those they teach. For you have written:

> *Since an overseer manages God's household, he must be blameless—not overbearing, not quick-tempered, not given to drunkenness, not violent, not pursuing dishonest gain. Rather, he must be hospitable, one who loves what is good, who is self-controlled, upright, holy and disciplined. He must hold firmly to the trustworthy message as it has been taught, so that he can encourage others by sound doctrine and refute those who oppose it. (Titus 1:7-9)*

This, no doubt, is a burden on the hearts of our pastors and a requirement impossible to fulfill through their own abilities. But you are the one who enables us to move mountains with the smallest faith,[3] and through Christ all things are possible[4] for us and our clergy.

Allow the Holy Spirit to come upon them so

In The Word

[1] *I Peter 2:25*

[2] *I Peter 5:4*

[3] *Matthew 17:20*

[4] *Philippians 4:13*

[5] *Ephesians 4:15*

[6] *Luke 15:3-7*

they will speak your words and not their own. Give them the compassion and wisdom to comfort those who are hurting, the leadership and knowledge to lead with vision, and the conviction to speak the truth in love.[5]

Above all, give them a heart for the lost and the broken. You are a shepherd who would leave your flock to find one sheep who's gone astray,[6] and I pray the vision of our pastors would mimic your heart for those who have been lost. There are those who do not know the danger they face; they do not know their Father is frantically searching for them. Give our pastors a heart for those whom you love so dearly.

And as you give our pastors a heart for the lost, give me a heart for my pastor. Guide me in prayer for him; give me the words to encourage and build him up. I pray the same prayer for our pastors and clergy that the author of Hebrews prayed:

> *Now may the God of peace, who through the blood of the eternal covenant brought back from the dead our Lord Jesus, that great Shepherd of the sheep, equip you with everything good for doing his will, and may he work in us what is pleasing to him, through Jesus Christ, to whom be glory for ever and ever. Amen. (Hebrews 13:20-21)*

And *AMEN*.

WEEK NINETEEN:

A Prayer for the American Church

Immanuel, your very name means "God with us,"[1] which I pray will be true for the church in America.

You have blessed our land with the freedom to worship, and I pray the lack of persecution we enjoy will not make us apathetic to the mission of your Kingdom. Burden our hearts for widows and orphans.[2] Create in us a desire to worship and serve the Lord[3] as we reach out to those in need. For you have called us to bare each other's burdens[4] and serve one another as an act of worship to our Lord:

> *"The King will reply, 'I tell you the truth,*
> *whatever you did for one of the least of these*
> *brothers of mine, you did for me.'"*
> *(Matthew 25:40)*

Help us realize the purpose of the church is not for our own satisfaction, but to fulfill your will in reaching the lost. To that end, let us equip ourselves through spiritual formation and sanctification not just for our personal growth, but to grow the body of Christ.[5]

Break our hearts for those who are lost and send your Holy Spirit to anoint us with the

In The Word

[1] *Matthew 1:23*

[2] *James 1:27*

[3] *Luke 4:8*

[4] *Galatians 6:2*

[5] *Ephesians 4:12*

[6] *Isaiah 61:1-3*

[7] *Revelation 2-3*

power to preach the good news to the poor, comfort those who mourn, lift up the broken hearted and bring freedom to those imprisoned by darkness.[6]

May the American church have a desire to see your name glorified above all things as we heed the words you wrote to the seven churches, saying:

> *He who has an ear, let him hear what the Spirit says to the churches. To him who overcomes, I will give the right to eat from the tree of life, which is in the paradise of God. (Revelation 2:7)*

May we in the American church reject evil and false teachings like the Church of Ephesus, but never lose our first love.
May we endure our suffering with faith like the church of Smyrna.
May we show love to others and remain true to your name like those in Pergamum and Thyatira, but reject immorality in the church.
May our church guard against being dead with only the façade of Christianity before us like the church of Sardis.
May we not be luke-warm in our faith like Laodicea, but instead be known for keeping your Word like the church of Philadelphia.[7]

I thank you for the freedom you've given us to speak your Word and worship your name. I give you the glory for our personal liberty in America and the eternal freedom we have through Christ.

May we in the American church be a reflection of your grace and compassion to those in need at all times.
   AMEN.

WEEK TWENTY:
A Call for Workers in the Harvest

L ord of the Harvest,[1] as I continue my prayer
for the American church, I ask you to give
us a singular focus on living missional lives:
lifestyles with a purpose of serving and
reaching others. You looked upon those without
a shepherd—those who were harassed and
helpless and said:

> *"The harvest is plentiful but the workers are
> few. Ask the Lord of the harvest, therefore, to
> send out workers into his harvest field."*
> *(Matthew 9:37-38)*

As you commanded, I ask for those workers to
be sent out. May your Holy Spirit reveal in my
heart what role you'd have me play; I ask this
not only for myself, but for each American
Christian.

Whether we consider ourselves missionaries to
our neighbors or to those in distant lands, give
us a heart for meeting the needs of others. For
you have called each of us to plant, water and
harvest the fields.

So often we do not see the opportunities for
ministry that are all around us. I ask you to
open our eyes to the harvest you've laid before

In The Word

[1] *Matthew 9:38*

[2] *John 4:35*

[3] *Mark 12:28-31*

us, for you have promised that the harvest is ready.[2]

Open our hearts to the mission of the church that we might see a great revival in America and throughout the world as you commanded saying:

> *"All authority in heaven and on earth has been given to me. Therefore go and make disciples of all nations, baptizing them in the name of the Father and of the Son and of the Holy Spirit, and teaching them to obey everything I have commanded you. And surely I am with you always, to the very end of the age."* *(Matthew 28:18-20)*

Above all, give us a heart for those who are lost and for those who have been sent into the harvest field. May we be moved to show love to our neighbor as we love our God, because you have called these the greatest commandments.[3]

AMEN.

Disciple Tip

PRAYING FOR MISSIONARIES

Each Christian is called to play a role in world missions. The Great Commission (Matthew 28:18-20) commands us to make disciples of every nation. God has blessed our country with the freedom of religion, but there are many Americans serving as missionaries where that's not the case. They are in constant danger for proclaiming the promise of freedom in Christ, and they deserve our prayers.

Most churches have particular missionaries they support. While those missionaries certainly need financial backing, we should also be engaged in their assignment. Choose a missionary family to support, but do more than just send a check—ask if they have a newsletter, send them letters from home, pray for them on a regular basis, research the area where they're serving, ask what you can do for their children. Supporting the workers God has placed around the world will make a big difference in the Kingdom.

WEEK TWENTY-ONE:
Prayer for the President's Cabinet

L ord of All,[1] you are the one who oversees our nation. You are the great advisor of our souls. As I continue to pray for our president, I also lift up those who advise him in the matters of our country.

May the Holy Spirit come upon those who serve in the president's cabinet with the gifts of leadership,[2] administration and wisdom,[3] so they might govern with diligence.

I pray you would give me a heart for the men and women who serve as the president's top advisors and as the heads of each executive department. Their counsel is vital to the success of our nation and our president:

For lack of guidance a nation falls,
but many advisers make victory sure.
(Proverbs 11:14)

Whether it be the Attorney General, the Secretary of State or any other cabinet position, I pray each member would seek your will both in their office and their lives.

Help me to remember them and their families in prayer as they serve our nation and

In The Word
[1] *Acts 10:36*

[2] *Romans 12:8*

[3] *I Corinthians 12*

[4] *Haggai 2:7*

our president.

I thank you for being our nation's greatest advisor and for the blessings you have given us. I pray you will be the desire of our nation, just as you will make yourself the desire of all nations.[4] I give you all the praise and glory.

    AMEN.

The Praying Patriot

PRAY THE NAMES

When praying for individuals in the government, it's important to use their names. While the prayer above represents a general prayer for the Cabinet as a whole, we must remember that we're actually praying for individual people, not their positions.

God puts a great deal of emphasis on people's names in the Bible; often our names define who we are. So whether we're praying for the members of the president's cabinet, our mayor, the governor or our local heroes, it's important to use their names. It will empower your prayer life and change your heart for them.

Use a prayer journal or the **Praying Patriot Worksheets** in the back of this book to remind yourself who you should be praying for, then specifically pray for them using their names and the names of their families.

WEEK TWENTY-TWO:

A Prayer for the Vice President

E ternal God,[1] you are the giver of this nation's hope. You are the one who sees the end as easily as the beginning,[2] and only you know what our future holds. Give us your wisdom in whatever trials or blessings may come to America.

Today I lift up our Vice President. Protect him as he presides over the Senate and counsels our president. May he be convicted by the Holy Spirit, who writes on the hearts of men, that he serves accountable not only to the president, but to the Lord who is our foundation.[3]

Give our Vice President a true heart for the nation and people he serves while remaining humble in his duties. For you have written:

Humility and fear of the LORD
bring wealth and honor and life.
(Proverbs 22:4)

May he seek your wisdom, fear any path that is not your will, and through those actions receive blessings and protection. May you be glorified in his life and position.
    AMEN.

"*God who gave us life gave us liberty. And can the liberties of a nation be thought secure when we have removed their only firm basis, a conviction in the minds of the people that these liberties are of the gift of God?*"

-*Thomas Jefferson*

PATRIOT QUOTE

WEEK TWENTY-THREE:

A Prayer for the Chief of Staff

C hief Shepherd,[1] you are worthy of praise.[2] May your name be glorified for all things good—for you are the leader of leaders and the shepherd of shepherds.

You, Lord, are the giver of administrative[3] and leadership[4] gifts, which the president's Chief of Staff needs in his position. I ask you to bestow these gifts on him as he manages the Executive Offices, aids the president and interacts with Congress.

Despite the great power wielded by his post, I confess I don't often remember the Chief of Staff in my prayers. But you have placed him in authority[5] over many, and like all men of power, he is in need of prayer.

We are separated from his day to day activities and his responsibilities are not often reported, but you see his heart and his actions. May the knowledge of that give him both comfort and divine accountability.

The President has given him command over all those who serve the executive branch. Is his position not similar to that of Joseph's when

In The Word

[1] *I Peter 5:4*

[2] *Psalm 18:3*

[3] *I Corinthians 12:28*

[4] *Romans 12:8*

[5] *Romans 13:1*

the king of Egypt said to him:

> *"You shall be in charge of my palace, and all my people are to submit to your orders. Only with respect to the throne will I be greater than you." (Genesis 41:40)*

May the Chief of Staff run his affairs with the same wisdom and integrity that you led Joseph, and may his heart be turned toward you in times of national trial.

　AMEN.

DiscipleTip

The Partisan Prayer

The primary weapon Satan uses against us is pride, and the greatest temptation when praying for our leaders is to pray with partisanship. Remember, God has a purpose for the life of our leaders—even when we don't agree with their policies. We are commanded to pray for our leaders so "we may live peaceful and quiet lives in all godliness and holiness. This is good, and pleases God our Savior, who wants all men to be saved and to come to a knowledge of the truth" (1 Timothy 2:2-4). While the command to pray for our leaders is clear, the motivation is sometimes lost. We are called to submit to the authorities over us (Romans 13:1) because the way we interact with the government is a witness to Christ's work in our lives. We must always be respectful of the office, even when we disagree with the policies coming out of it. Here are some additional tips to help:

- Ask God to reveal your motives; be sure you're praying for God's will in the lives of our leaders and not your own.
- Concentrate your prayers on their protection and family lives. That's not to say you can't pray for policy, but remember that you're praying for your God-established leader, not your enemy.
- Purposefully pray for politicians who serve outside your own political party.
- Never engage in negative talk about our leaders. Discussing policy is one thing, but disrespecting our leaders dishonors God.
- Though we hear pundits do it all the time, never refer to our president or representatives by their last name alone. There's technically nothing wrong with referring to "Bush" or "Obama" from a news perspective, but we're called to be more than technically accurate. Show respect for the office by always including the title of the individual—President or Senator.

Remember, prayer is never about changing someone else; it's always about allowing God to change us.

WEEK TWENTY-FOUR:

Prayer for the Secretary of State

Desired One of All Nations,[1] you look down upon the earth without boundaries, for all the earth belongs to you.[2] You are the one who judges the earth, for every nation is your inheritance.[3]

We leave these judgments in your hands, but though your Kingdom is without borders, we live in a fallen world of boundaries and war. Show us your will as we relate with other nations, and bring wisdom to those whose burden it is to make diplomatic decisions.

I lift up the heart, mind and soul of our Secretary of State. May she seek the Holy Spirit's approval in every interaction she has with foreign leaders. May she see your light when advising the president in our darkest hours.

May she lead us in advancing the cause of freedom and meeting the needs of the international community with integrity and godly compassion.

But may we also be protected from becoming indistinguishable from other nations.

In The Word

[1] *Haggai 2:7*

[2] *Deuteronomy 10:14*

[3] *Psalm 82:8*

[4] *Philippians 4:7*

Set us apart to do your work in the world, even at the
expense of being unpopular. Do not allow us to be like the Israelites
of the past who rejected your call to be a light to the nations when
you spoke of them:

> *"You say, 'We want to be like the nations, like the peoples of the*
> *world, who serve wood and stone.' But what you have in mind*
> *will never happen. As surely as I live, declares the Sovereign*
> *Lord, I will rule over you with a mighty hand and an outstretched*
> *arm and with outpoured wrath." (Ezekiel 20:32-33)*

Give us a desire to seek your approval above the approval of other
nations and protect us from the judgment we would bring upon
ourselves for abandoning you.

Our Secretary of State faces seemingly impossible decisions on a
daily basis. She must deal with one country in a manner that will
offend another, and her choices have world-wide implications. I pray
you grant her rest and a peace that transcends all understanding[4] as
you guide her through the burdens and achievements of diplomacy.

Bring her success in her charge and blessings to our nations.
May we be a light to other nations in your will.
   AMEN.

WEEK TWENTY-FIVE:
Prayer for the Secretary of Defense

Defender and Protector, you are our strength and our shield.[1] We need not be afraid, for you see when a single sparrow falls and have counted the very hairs on our head.[2] You put your arms of protection around us.

I pray for the heavy heart of our Secretary of Defense and his team. He carries an immense burden that I cannot fully understand or appreciate. He has been charged with the protection of a nation, which is something man cannot provide without your favor.

Is there another in our nation who more fully needs to prepare himself with the armor of God? I pray then, that he seeks you in his cause and is driven to the words you spoke to the Ephesians:

> *Stand firm then, with the belt of truth buckled around your waist, with the breastplate of righteousness in place, and with your feet fitted with the readiness that comes from the gospel of peace.*
> *(Ephesians 6:14-15)*

Give our Secretary of Defense the grounding that comes from your truth, the blessings that come from your righteousness and the peace that comes from knowing your gospel, even in the darkest moments of our nation's history. Let him also:

> *take up the shield of faith, with which you can extinguish all the flaming arrows of the evil one. Take the helmet of salvation and the sword of the Spirit, which is the word of God. And pray in the Spirit on all occasions with all kinds of prayers and requests. (Ephesians 6:16-18)*

May his faith be strengthened, his salvation be assured, and though he has many weapons and armies at his disposal, may he hold the sword of your Word above them all.

Although my burdens are not the same, I too represent both America and your Kingdom with my actions. Reveal the changes that are required in my own heart to fully wear this armor, and may I be used as an instrument of your grace and mercy. Let each of us put the faith of our defense in you, for your very name is a tower of strength.[3] May your name be glorified.

AMEN.

WEEK TWENTY-SIX:

A Prayer for the C.I.A.

G reat Father, you command the mighty winds, the earthquakes and fire. But you are also found as a Gentle Whisper.[1] I praise you for both the truth your Holy Spirit reveals[2] and the mysteries that are kept until the end of days.[3] Only you know what wisdom should be revealed. Your ways are holy, but the hearts of men must be guarded.

I pray for those who defend our nation through the necessity of information and secrecy. I do not covet the responsibility that befalls them. May they be accountable to the Most High, and seek your favor in the integrity of their work:

> *For the Lord grants wisdom!*
> *From his mouth come knowledge and*
> *understanding. He grants a treasure of*
> *common sense to the honest. He is a shield*
> *to those who walk with integrity. He*
> *guards the paths of the just and protects*
> *those who are faithful to him.*
> *(Proverbs 2:6-8, NLT)*

In that truth, give our CIA leaders access to the wisdom and intelligence necessary to protect our land. Let them see that the beginning of knowledge comes from a fear of the Lord.[4]
AMEN.

In The Word

[1] *I Kings 19:11-12*

[2] *John 16:13*

[3] *Daniel 12:4*

[4] *Proverbs 1:7*

> "The race is not to the swift, nor the battle to the strong; but the God of Israel is He that giveth strength and power unto His people. Trust in Him at all times, ye people, pour out your hearts before Him; God is a refuge for us."
>
> *-Abigail Adams*

PATRIOT QUOTE

WEEK TWENTY-SEVEN:

A Prayer for the F.B.I.

S un of Righteousness, you have promised to bring justice upon those who are wicked and bring healing to those who revere your name.[1] You alone are the source of all justice, knowledge and peace.

In The Word

[1] *Malachi 4:1-3*

[2] *Psalm 140:12*

[3] *Deuteronomy 10:18*

I pray a blessing on those who serve to bring earthly justice, knowledge and peace to the victims of crime in our land. Give them, both agent and administrative staff, the heart to see what can only be revealed by the Holy Spirit.

I ask that you would be with each agent, whether looking for a missing child, tracking terrorist plots, fighting organized crime or protecting us against fraud. Do not allow their hearts to be hardened by the harsh world they see, but strengthened by showing compassion to those who need it:

> *This is what the LORD Almighty says: Administer true justice; show mercy and compassion to one another. (Zachariah 7:9)*

You have promised to maintain the cause of the afflicted,[2] and I trust you will administer justice for the fatherless and the widows.[3]

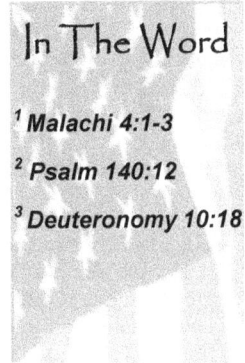

You are worthy of praise. Your justice is greater than any that can be found on earth, but I lift up those in the FBI who serve to protect our country and bring peace to the victims of crime. Strengthen and encourage them.

　　AMEN.

The Praying Patriot

Praying for Government Agencies

The FBI is one of the federal government's most diverse agencies. Its agents fight terrorism but also work child abduction cases. The varied nature of their job can make it difficult to know how to pray for them, but you don't necessarily need to pray for everything the FBI does. Familiarize yourself with the types of crime the FBI defends against, then pray for those specific areas of its mission the Holy Spirit puts on your heart. A visit to the agency website can help you identify the types of work agents do. Here's a partial list of what their site identifies as things the FBI investigates:

- International and Domestic Terrorism
- Counterintelligence
- Economic Espionage
- Online Predators
- Internet Fraud
- Identity Theft
- Government and Election Fraud
- Foreign Corrupt Practices
- Human Trafficking
- Organized Crime
- Corporate Securities Fraud
- Insurance Fraud
- Art Theft
- Bank Robbery
- Money Laundering

Learn more about what the FBI does by visiting www.fbi.gov. This technique can also be used when praying for other government agencies as well. Remember, the more specific our prayers, the more we'll be able to connect with God in an intimate way.

WEEK TWENTY-EIGHT:

A Prayer for the Secret Service

S hield of Abram,[1] you are the great protector. You, the King of kings, left your throne to stand between your children and the wages of sin, which is death.[2] You have called us your friends,[3] and have given your life to protect us:

In The Word

[1] *Genesis 15:1*

[2] *Romans 6:23*

[3] *John 15:14*

[4] *John 14:16*

> *Greater love has no one than this, that he lay down his life for his friends.*
> *(John 15:13)*

It is a rare man who will lay down his life for another. We see that dedication in the lives of our troops and again in the lives of our Secret Service agents. They serve without recognition or appreciation, willing to step between our public officials and death. Paul wrote of Christ:

> *You see, at just the right time, when we were still powerless, Christ died for the ungodly. Very rarely will anyone die for a righteous man, though for a good man someone might possibly dare to die. But God demonstrates his own love for us in this: While we were still sinners, Christ died for us. (Romans 5:6-8)*

You sacrificed your life for me regardless of what I had done. You fulfilled your promise of salvation even when I was unworthy.

Your mercy and grace cannot be compared, but I lift up those who serve our country with a heart of sacrifice. They are willing to stand between our officials and danger, and they do so free of judgment toward their policies or lifestyles. They bring stability to our nation.

I pray also for the families of our Secret Service agents. While I rest, they spend sleepless nights concerned for the safety of their loved ones. This too is a sacrifice for our country. You see their suffering and I ask you to send the Holy Spirit to bring them comfort.[4] Bring blessings to their households and protection to our protectors.
    AMEN.

WEEK TWENTY-NINE:
A Prayer for Veterans Affairs

M erciful God,[1] may your compassion and
grace continue to fall on those troops who
serve our country and the veterans who
have served before them.

Your Word honors those who serve with
integrity—the Centurion of great faith who
called on your authority,[2] your promise of land
to Caleb after forty-five years of service[3] and
the faith of Cornelius[4]—all these passages speak
of honored soldiers.

I pray now for our veterans and those working
in the Department of Veterans Affairs. Give
them the discernment to fairly honor those who
have served our country with distinction.

Do not allow us, as a nation, to forget those who
have sacrificed so much for our freedom. Allow
us to honor their service with the same integrity
they served us. Whether their scars be physical,
emotional, or originate from a lonely heart, do
not allow our country to forget them.

Give the Secretary of Veterans Affairs a true
heart for veterans and their stories. Allow his
post to be a mission of compassion, and

In The Word

[1] *Jeremiah 3:12*

[2] *Matthew 8:5-10*

[3] *Joshua 14:6-15*

[4] *Acts 10:1-4*

[5] *John 14:16*

not simply a job of administrative finances.

But as we honor our veterans, send the Holy Spirit to be their primary councilor.[5] For true reward does not come from the government or its citizenry. True reward and honor comes only from the Most High. Allow our veterans to seek your righteousness so they might claim the words of Paul, who wrote:

> *I have fought the good fight, I have finished the race, I have kept the faith. Now there is in store for me the crown of righteousness, which the Lord, the righteous Judge, will award to me on that day—and not only to me, but also to all who have longed for his appearing. (2 Timothy 4:7-8)*

Change also my own heart, that I may see those who have sacrificed through your eyes. Let me seek only your reward and remain faithful only to you.

AMEN.

WEEK THIRTY:

A Prayer for Homeland Security

ternal God, you are our refuge. You drive out the enemies of the faithful.[1] Thank you for your protection from those who seek to do evil against us.

In The Word

[1] *Deuteronomy 33:27*

[2] *Psalm 18:9*

[3] *Isaiah 46:10*

I pray for those who labor in the Department of Homeland Security. Let them also take refuge in your name as they secure our nation from both foreign and domestic threats.

Whether fighting terrorism, safeguarding government computer systems, enforcing safe immigration laws or responding to disasters, may the Secretary of Homeland Security and her team be given the gift of wisdom. May they have access to the information they need while still preserving our freedom with integrity.

As I pray for their wisdom and discernment, I also ask for an awakening in our country. May that revival bring back to the forefront our desire to have you as our defender and strength.[2]

May we remember that true security only comes from your continued favor on our nation. Let us cry out in one voice:

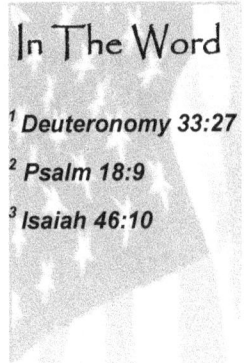

The LORD is my rock, my fortress and my deliverer;
my God is my rock, in whom I take refuge.
He is my shield and the horn of my salvation, my stronghold.
I call to the LORD, who is worthy of praise,
and I am saved from my enemies.
(Psalm 18:2-3)

Protect our nation and do not turn your favor away from us. You are the God who makes known the end from the beginning.[3] You know the plots against our people and how that information can make its way to the authorities you've anointed. Let us seek your knowledge, grace and protection.

   AMEN.

WEEK THIRTY-ONE:
A Prayer for NASA

C reator of the heavens and earth,[1] as you knit together our innermost beings within the wombs of our mothers,[2] you placed in us a desire to learn and ask questions. You gave us a desire to explore your creation.

The mission of NASA has given us new wonder and perspective on your glory. You did not create the universe with a simplicity that could be grasped, but as a mysterious gift we continue to discover. Its very complexity is a testimony to your majesty:

> *The heavens proclaim the glory of God.*
> *The skies display his craftsmanship.*
> *Day after day they continue to speak;*
> *night after night they make him known.*
> *They speak without a sound or word;*
> *their voice is never heard.*
> *Yet their message has gone throughout the*
> *earth, and their words to all the world.*
> *(Psalm 19:1-4, NLT)*

You created the earth with your power, founded the world with your wisdom and expanded the heavens with your knowledge.[3]

I pray for continued revelation through your creation and that the mission of NASA will

In The Word

[1] *Genesis 1:1*

[2] *Psalm 139:13*

[3] *Jeremiah 51:15*

[4] *Romans 1:25*

prosper from a desire to see your hand in all things. But do not allow us to become like those who Paul admonished. May we never lose our focus on your glory and exchange the truth of creation for a lie. Do not allow us to worship the creation over the Creator.[4] For your creation is a testament to your sovereignty and we are held accountable for acknowledging your glory:

> *For since the creation of the world God's invisible qualities—his eternal power and divine nature—have been clearly seen, being understood from what has been made, so that men are without excuse. (Romans 1:20)*

Instead, let us use our natural desire for knowledge to seek you. May you bless those who have seen your greatness through the advances of NASA and may we be continually filled with wonder by the majesty of your creation.

> *AMEN.*

—————————————— Disciple Tip

GOD'S CREATION

As Psalm 19 tells us, creation is the greatest proof of God's existence. The universe is far too complex to have been created by random events. If you want to understand the grandeur and majesty of God, begin by studying his creation—both scientifically and biblically. Science is not the enemy of God; it was originally established to seek God. Here are just a few additional verses to help you get started:

- Genesis 1:1- 2:25
- John 1:1-3, 10-14
- Psalm 8:1-9
- 1 Corinthians 15:40-41
- Revelation 4:9-11

Also, consider an in-depth study of the Book of Job with your small group. There are many insights about creation throughout the entire book. An easier way to begin is by taking a walk; take time to see the majesty of God's creation all around you. Then ask the Holy Spirit to reveal the truth of scripture as you read the Word.

WEEK THIRTY-TWO:
A Call to Worship

I mmanuel,[1] should we not rejoice because you stand beside us? Have we, as a nation, forgotten your very name means that you are with us? Have we forgotten your promise to be with us until the end of the age?[2] Should we not glorify your name after having our nation shaped by the blessings of your hand?

Call our people into sincere worship! For you have promised to draw near to those who draw near to you.[3] Let our songs of praise echo into the world as a witness to the nations:

> *Hear this, you kings! Listen, you rulers!*
> *I will sing to the LORD, I will sing;*
> *I will make music to the LORD, the God of*
> *Israel. (Judges 5:3)*

Like Moses, who stood before you in worship, let others be drawn into song as the Spirit calls them through our praise.[4] You are worthy.

May we never forget the gifts you have bestowed on our country. Do not let us grumble like the Israelites who rejected your promise,[5] but let our eyes be open to the great things you have given America. May we attribute our prosperity to your favor and glory, that we

In The Word

[1] *Isaiah 7:14*

[2] *Matthew 28:20*

[3] *James 4:8*

[4] *Exodus 33:9-10*

[5] *Numbers 14:1-4*

might be a witness to the world, saying:

> *You turned my wailing into dancing;*
> *you removed my sackcloth and clothed me with joy,*
> *that my heart may sing to you and not be silent.*
> *O Lord my God, I will give you thanks forever.*
> *(Psalm 30:11-12)*

The strength of America is in your favor alone.

May we not be ashamed to call out your name.

May we not be afraid to speak your truth.

May we not be embarrassed to sing your praises.

Let us not be shackled so we may dance.

>   *AMEN.*

WEEK THIRTY-THREE:

A Prayer for our Entertainers

L ight of the World,[1] may we be drawn always
to the glory of *your* radiance, Creator of the
heavens, and not the stars we have created
for ourselves.

I am grateful for our entertainers. You have
gifted them with song, drama and dance. You
have given us a land where artists can prosper.
The arts bring joy and perspective. They change
the way we view the world and can bring glory
to your creation.

But have we made idols of our entertainers?
Are they at all different from Israel's golden
calf? Are we responsible; have we destroyed
them like the gold Aaron placed into the fire?[2]

I lift up our entertainers and celebrities to you.
May they recognize the power they have over
our society and take that responsibility
seriously. Give them an inner strength that they
may not be consumed by the altar of worship
we've placed them on.

May we devote the arts to glorifying your name.
For even as Paul quoted the entertainers of his
day,[3] he warned against worshiping idols.

In The Word

[1] *John 8:12*

[2] *Exodus 32:1-4*

[3] *Acts 17:28*

Are we not responsible for creating these American idols? You have given us these gifts to enjoy, but you have also warned us:

> *See to it that no one takes you captive through hollow and deceptive philosophy, which depends on human tradition and the basic principles of this world rather than on Christ. (Colossians 2:8)*

May we be cautious not to destroy those whom you've gifted with our adoration. Let us treat our entertainers with the respect their talent deserves, but stop short of letting those talents distract us from worshipping you, who created them.

AMEN.

DiscipleTip

PRAYING FOR CELEBRITIES

Who wants to pray for celebrities? Their lives are so much better than ours and their problems are their own making, right? How many times have we said something like, "If I had the money and fame she had, I wouldn't act like that!"

Maybe we wouldn't, but can we be sure of that? Entertainers and sports figures have been put into a place of worship by our society and then we condemn them for falling short of God's perfection. Don't get me wrong, celebrities are responsible for their own actions, but we're often responsible for pushing them to those actions—whether by stress or entitlement.

The basis of this book is to pray for those in authority over us, and like it or not, we've put celebrities in a place of authority. When a teen singer is arrested, maybe we should pray for them without prejudice rather than touting what better celebrities we'd make

It's a difficult transition to make, but what impact would it have on your children's lives if they saw you praying for the protection and wisdom of the entertainers they follow?

WEEK THIRTY-FOUR:

A Prayer for our Sports Heroes

S trength of our Lives,[1] you are mighty to save,[2] and I give you glory! You are the standard by which excellence is measured. May your name be glorified among our sports figures as they seek excellence in their profession.

In The Word

[1] *Psalm 27:1*

[2] *Isaiah 63:1*

[3] *2 Samuel 11:14-15*

[4] *Numbers 20:1-12*

[5] *Mark 14:66-72*

Your Word holds the discipline of sports in high regard. It often serves as an example of strong Christian living:

> *Everyone who competes in the games goes into strict training. They do it to get a crown that will not last; but we do it to get a crown that will last forever.*
> *(1 Corinthians 9:25)*

And while the trophies of our sports heroes will perish, the athletes make a lasting impression on our society. Give them a sense of accountability for that influence.

The men whom we call heroes of the Bible were flawed—David committed murder,[3] Moses lashed out in anger against your command,[4] and Peter denied knowing you.[5] Today's sports heroes are also flawed, but inspire the nation with their excellence.

Give them peace in the pressures of life and protect them from temptation.

May their training and skill bring you glory, and may they be spared from corruption by pride and public adulation.

    AMEN.

WEEK THIRTY-FIVE:

A Prayer for our News Media

ather God, I have called on you to make us a people of worship—to turn our exaltation away from celebrities and sports figures. I now lift up the individuals of our news media, who influence our perception of the world.

In The Word

[1] *Galatians 5:1*

[2] *Psalm 25:5*

[3] *Acts 17:11*

You have given us freedom in Christ[1] to protect us from the oppression of death. Our nation was founded with freedom of the press to protect us from the oppression of government without bias.

I pray now for the integrity of our news media. Have facts given way to opinion? Have we truly embraced the lie that truth is subjective? Have we lost our ability to seek truth without predisposition? I pray that it would not be so. For you have called us to be led by truth.[2]

Just as Paul wrote to the Ephesians, give members of our news media a desire for truth:

> *Therefore each of you must put off falsehood and speak truthfully to his neighbor, for we are all members of one body. (Ephesians 4:25)*

Do not let us, as Christians, be swayed by the

opinions of either side, but search the scriptures daily to discern what is true.[3]

I am grateful that we have free speech—I am thankful that we have freedom of the press and that the government does not control the words of man. But the media, like all industries, is run by flawed individuals. I pray for a renewed quest for truth in our society, and especially in our news media.

To those who seek truth and put themselves in harm's way to report what they have uncovered, I pray that you would bring them protection and blessings.

   AMEN.

WEEK THIRTY-SIX:

A Prayer for our Farmers

L ord of the Harvest,[1] you have created the
earth and filled it with all manner of food
for us to cultivate. You created every plant
and animal to sustain us,[2] and there is not a
man on earth who does not need the farmer to
nourish him:

In The Word

[1] *Matthew 9:38*

[2] *Genesis 1:29-30*

[3] *Genesis 3:17-19*

[4] *Matthew 13:1-23*

[5] *Luke 13:6-8*

[6] *Romans 11:24*

[7] *Revelation 14:15*

[8] *Matthew 3:12*

> *The increase from the land is taken by all;*
> *the king himself profits from the fields.*
> *(Ecclesiastes 5:9)*

But since the fall of man, husbandry requires
long and difficult labor.[3] For this reason, I lift
up the American farmer in prayer.

Many of us have lost our connection to the toil
from which our food comes. We see our
abundant prosperity come by truck to our
overstocked supermarkets without a thought
toward the farmer who labors desperately to
save the land of his forefathers.

Forgive me for my arrogance. I have received
the reward of America's success without
attributing that prosperity to you and those
who work your fields.

The patriarchs of Israel and the forefathers of

America understood their connection to your provision through farming. They plowed the land and raised animals for food.

So much of your Word is conveyed through husbandry. Your instruction and commandments are expressed through the concepts of sowing,[4] fertilizing,[5] grafting,[6] reaping[7] and winnowing.[8] Do not let us become so disconnected from the work of our farmers that we lose our ability to grasp your Word.

May our farmers be blessed with security and prosperity. Teach us to be mindful of their efforts as we support them with thanksgiving and gratitude.

AMEN.

WEEK THIRTY-SEVEN:
A Prayer for our Fishermen

M aker of the Fishers of Men,[1] you befriended the fisherman from the very beginning of your ministry on earth. I pray now for those in America who maintain that ancient occupation of provision.

In The Word

[1] *Matthew 4:19*

[2] *Genesis 1:26*

[3] *Psalm 104:25*

You have given us dominion over the fish of the sea[2] and I am grateful for those who provide us with your gifts.

Whether by hook off the coast of Cape Cod, nets in the Gulf of Mexico or pots in the Bearing Sea, fishing is one of the most dangerous jobs in our nation. I pray a blessing of protection on these men and women. They provide for our families while being away from their own.

Let them seek your provision and wisdom as they fish. By their faith, may your glory be revealed in the bounty of their nets, just as in Peter's:

> *Early in the morning, Jesus stood on the shore, but the disciples did not realize that it was Jesus. He called out to them, "Friends, haven't you any fish?" "No," they answered. He said, "Throw your net on the right side of the boat and you*

will find some." When they did, they were unable to haul the net in because of the large number of fish. (John 21:4-6)

Bring this blessing on our fishermen as well. Do not let us take for granted the great bounty you have provided in the rivers and oceans. For their species are innumerable[3] and you are the giver of life.
   AMEN.

WEEK THIRTY-EIGHT:
A Prayer for our Workforce

In The Word

[1] *Isaiah 64:8*

[2] *Colossians 3:23*

[3] *Matthew 6:24*

[4] *1 Corinthians 12*

Lord God, you are the potter and have fashioned us like clay[1] to be individuals who serve. You have created each one of us with unique gifts and talents. Like those chosen to build the tabernacle, you have created us to do a specific task:

> *[God] has filled them with skill to do all kinds of work as craftsmen, designers, embroiderers in blue, purple and scarlet yarn and fine linen, and weavers—all of them master craftsmen and designers. (Exodus 35:35)*

I pray for the workforce of America, who are the backbone of our nation. Do not allow them to be discouraged. Instead, give them the encouragement you gave Solomon through David:

> *"Be strong and courageous, and do the work. Do not be afraid or discouraged, for the LORD God, my God, is with you. He will not fail you or forsake you until all the work for the service of the temple of the LORD is finished." (1 Chronicles 28:20)*

Let us also be reminded that, like Solomon, we are called to serve you, not man. Every hardship we face in the workplace should be met with the remembrance that we work for your sake,[2] not the sake of others—for no one can serve two masters.[3]

Lift up American workers and strengthen their resolve. Do not allow them to be downtrodden or oppressed. Let them seek you and your purpose in their lives. You have put a desire in their hearts and prepared them with spiritual gifts to be used in their service and work.[4]

Bring a revival of purpose and encouragement to the workforce of our country. May our labor bring you glory and strengthen America's economy.
   AMEN.

WEEK THIRTY-NINE:
A Prayer for our Infrastructure

F ather God, the makeup of any modern civilization is based on its infrastructure: roads, bridges, rails and waterways. Would the gospel have reached so many without Paul's access to Roman roads?

How many discoveries of your Word were found in travel? Compassion was found on the road to Jericho.[1] The hope of your resurrection was found on the road to Emmaus,[2] and Paul's salvation was found on the road to Damascus.[3]

Do not let us neglect our own infrastructure; the safety and connection of our communities depend on it.

Lives are changed by the infrastructure of a nation. It brings families together, provides commerce and allows the movement of supplies in times of disaster.

I confess that I have taken these things for granted. Our generation has forgotten how difficult it once was to travel. Protect our roads and bridges. Give us an appreciation for the ease of travel we enjoy.
    AMEN.

In The Word

[1] *Luke 10:30-37*

[2] *Luke 24:13-35*

[3] *Acts 9:1-19*

The Praying Patriot

PRAYING FOR A BRIDGE IS BORING

Praying for America's infrastructure doesn't seem very exciting. There's not many churches hosting regular prayer meetings for roads and bridges, but that's because we take our infrastructure for granted. That's something many Vermont residents no longer do—not after tropical storm Irene devastated much of the state in 2011.

According to Scott Neuman's August 30, 2011 article, *Flooding From Irene Damages Roads, Strands Towns*, on NPR's website, "Vermont Gov. Peter Shumlin said Irene triggered the worst flooding the state has seen in a century as the storm moved north into Canada. At least 260 roads were impassable, and 30 bridges were either down or deemed unsafe."

The loss of those roads and bridges left a dozen communities completely cut off from the rest of the state. Helicopters were used to bring in food and supplies. I personally know someone who was rescued from their second story window by boat because the roads were gone. The storm caused devastation all along the Mid-Atlantic and Northeast regions of the nation. Suddenly, we didn't take our infrastructure for granted any longer.

It's easy to become complacent about our power supplies, roadways and bridges, but incidents like Irene in 2011, the effects of Hurricane Katrina on the Gulf Coast in 2005, and the Minnesota bridge that collapsed over the Mississippi in 2007 remind us how easy it would be for us to become cut off from the rest of the world.

It may not be the most glamorous of prayers, but it is important for us to keep America's infrastructure at the forefront of our minds. We should bring these things before God in prayer and be engaged with our local representatives to be sure our infrastructure remains safe.

WEEK FORTY:
A Prayer for Israel

R edeemer and Holy One of Israel,[1] for the
sake of your blessing on America, I lift up
Jerusalem and Israel in prayer. It is your
nation, for you established it as a covenant with
Abraham.[2] You have promised blessings on
those who bless Israel and a curse on those who
turn away from it.[3]

You are holy, and have commanded us to pray
for the security and prosperity of Jerusalem,
saying:

> *Pray for peace in Jerusalem.*
> *May all who love this city prosper.*
> *O Jerusalem, may there be peace within*
> *your walls and prosperity in your palaces.*
> *For the sake of my family and friends, I*
> *will say, "May you have peace."*
> *(Psalm 122:6-8 NLT)*

Like David, I pray for the sake of my family,
friends and nation.

To be a follower of the Messiah, I must have a
heart for the things of his heart. My Lord wept
for Jerusalem,[4] and will one day rebuild the city
where he'll reign forever.[5]

Until that day, I pray for the protection and

In The Word

[1] *Isaiah 49:7*

[2] *Genesis 12:2*

[3] *Genesis 12:3*

[4] *Luke 19:41*

[5] *Revelation 21:1-4*

security of Israel—for its peace, that America might be blessed.

Lord, bring security to your people,
and security to the United States.
Bring peace to the nation of Abraham,
and peace to America.
Bring blessings to the people of Israel,
and blessings to our nation for our obedience.
   AMEN.

--- Disciple Tip

WHY AM I PRAYING FOR ISRAEL?

I thought this book was about America?! Why are there three prayers devoted to Israel and the Jewish people?

Israel is a hot-button topic—there's no doubt about it. Some will undoubtedly be offended by this section of the book, but the Bible is very clear: Those who bless Israel will be blessed (Genesis 12:3) and nations who persecute Israel will be cursed (Deuteronomy 30:7). God has blessed America beyond comprehension, and much of that is derived from our support of Israel.

Does that mean we're forced to agree with everything the Israeli government does? Does it mean we're without sovereignty regarding Israel's political decisions? Certainly not. We, as a nation, are accountable to God, not Israel. But because we're accountable to God, we must follow his commands and respect his covenants. While we may not always agree with Israel, we are called to pray for the nation and be their political allies.

One of the Enemy's greatest lies is that God abandoned Israel in favor of the church, but Paul speaks for three chapters in the book of Romans about God's relationship with the Jews culminating in his promise to restore Israel at the end of the church age (Romans 11:25). The fulfillment of his promise has already begun. How is it possible that a nation could survive without a country for a thousand years, only to be restored to its land a millennium after being scattered? It is only possible with God. Any doubt of God's commitment to Israel should have been dissolved upon Israel's reinstatement in 1948.

For the sake of America, pray for Israel—pray for the Jewish people.

WEEK FORTY-ONE:
A Prayer for the Jewish People

G od of Abraham, Isaac and Jacob,[1] you are
the consolation of Israel;[2] the children of
Abraham have been scattered across the
nations[3] and I pray for their blessing—those
who live on foreign soil and especially those in
America. You have not abandoned your people,
for Paul wrote:

> *Israel has experienced a hardening in part
> until the full number of the Gentiles has
> come in. And so all Israel will be saved, as
> it is written:*
> *"The deliverer will come from Zion;*
> *he will turn godlessness away from Jacob.*
> *And this is my covenant with them*
> *when I take away their sins."*
> *(Romans 11:25-27)*

The Enemy has toiled to destroy your people,
but as with Joseph's redemption, what Satan
intended for evil you will use for good.[4] I pray
for those children of Jacob who have suffered,
and ask that your hand of protection might be
upon them until they are fully assembled again
under your banner:

> *This is what the Sovereign LORD says: I
> will gather you from the nations and bring
> you back from the countries where you*

have been scattered, and I will give you back the land of Israel again.' (Ezekiel 11:17)

May the Jewish people of America, with their Christian brothers and sisters, find security without persecution here. May they find freedom without oppression and peace without intolerance. May their eyes be unveiled to the fulfillment of the Messiah's appearing.

Your grace is sufficient,[5] and your covenant is irrevocable.[6]
Praise the God of Abraham, the God of Isaac and the God of Jacob. As you have commanded, may you be known by this name from generation to generation forever.[7]

   AMEN.

WEEK FORTY-TWO:
A Prayer for Israeli Relations

aithful and True God,[1] I pray for the relationship between America and Israel. For you have promised to bless those who love Israel and curse those who curse the children of Abraham.[2]

In The Word

[1] *Revelation 19:11*

[2] *Genesis 12:3*

[3] *Genesis 15:17-20*

I especially lift up the U.S. Ambassador to Israel and our Secretary of State. May they be guided by your wisdom and seek your desire in each interaction with Israel.

Help our nation to discern your will, and support Israel when it is aligned with your will. Above all, do not let us forget Israel. Do not allow us to abandon its friendship—for you have said of Israel:

> *The LORD your God will put all these curses on your enemies who hate and persecute you. (Deuteronomy 30:7)*

Give us a sense of brotherhood with Israel, for the same God who blessed America personally established the Jewish nation.[3] Grant us an understanding of your purpose in our relations with Israel. May your name be glorified through the United States and the House of Jacob.
AMEN.

"*America was founded by people who believed that God was their rock of safety. I recognize we must be cautious in claiming that God is on our side, but I think it's all right to keep asking if we're on His side.*"

-Ronald Reagan

PATRIOT QUOTE

WEEK FORTY-THREE:

A Prayer for an American Revival

L iving Redeemer,[1] having blessed the people of Israel as you commanded,[2] I ask you to bless us with a revival of your Holy Spirit in the United States.

You have called us to have a heart for missions. You have commanded us to spread the gospel throughout the world, saying:

> *"Therefore go and make disciples of all nations, baptizing them in the name of the Father and of the Son and of the Holy Spirit, and teaching them to obey everything I have commanded you. And surely I am with you always, to the very end of the age." (Matthew 28:19-20)*

Today I turn my prayers back to the unbelieving of America. Let us also be missionaries to our own nation!

We, as a people, humble ourselves in prayer and ask for the opportunity to be healed.[3] Send the Holy Spirit into our land; send him to convict the hearts of those who need your salvation,[4] and guide believers to witness with actions of love.[5] Let your children be known for their gentleness and respect—not their judgment.[6] Through these things,

In The Word

[1] *Job 19:25*

[2] *Psalm 122:6*

[3] *2 Chronicles 7:14*

[4] *John 16:8*

[5] *Matthew 22:39*

[6] *1 Peter 3:15*

I pray for a true revival in America.

I have prayed for those in authority over us that we might have stability in our nation; may the body of Christ not squander that stability or the freedoms we've been afforded. Instead, may the Holy Spirit convict us with a heart for the lost. Give us a desire to feed the hungry, clothe the needy, and fight for the oppressed. These are the duties of the church. Should it be said that a nation cares more for its people than the followers of Christ? Never. Rather, the actions of the church should show God's heart of compassion.

You are worthy of service! You are worthy of sacrifice!
Change the heart of American Christians so we might do more than pray for revival; change us so we might live a revival into being.
    AMEN.

WEEK FORTY-FOUR:
A Call to Financial Stewardship

B read of Life,[1] you are my true provider. Your grace is sufficient,[2] and I give you praise! You have promised to meet all my needs according to the riches of Jesus Christ![3]

We, however, have become a nation that does not embrace that promise. Instead, we have sought our own pleasures, depending on un-payable debt to meet our desires.

Despite your warning that the borrower is slave to the lender,[4] we have buried ourselves in debt at both an individual and national level. Forgive us for our sin, and let us heed your admonition:

Do not be a man who strikes hands in pledge or puts up security for debts; if you lack the means to pay, your very bed will be snatched from under you.
(Proverbs 22:26-27)

Instead, you have said:

Let no debt remain outstanding, except the continuing debt to love one another, for he who loves his fellowman has fulfilled the law. (Romans 13:8)

Make us, again, a people who trust in you to provide. Remind us that all wealth belongs to

In The Word

[1] *John 6:35*

[2] *2 Corinthians 12:9*

[3] *Philippians 4:19*

[4] *Proverbs 22:7*

[5] *Haggai 2:8*

you alone,[5] and we are responsible for our stewardship of your possessions. Do not allow us to be greedy, but generous.

Teach us to hold our households and our politicians accountable for being godly stewards of your resources. Open our eyes to the shackles in which we've bound ourselves. Help us to declare freedom from the slavery we've sold ourselves into.

Teach us to obey your will, for you have promised to prosper those who love you:

> *If they obey and serve him,*
> *they will spend the rest of their days in prosperity*
> *and their years in contentment. (Job 36:11)*

AMEN.

--- DiscipleTip

HOPE IN FINANCIAL FREEDOM

One of the most difficult aspects of American Christianity is stewardship. Our sense of individualism combined with cultural norms makes trusting God with our wallets the final frontier of spiritual health.

Many people believe they'll never be able to live without debt—they've been fooled into thinking their shackles are unbreakable, but it's not true! God lays out a clear path to financial freedom and if you need help, my wife and I strongly recommend Dave Ramsey's Financial Peace University.

When a man named Greg Tkach brought FPU to our church, Gina and I had $80,000.00 in non-mortgage related debt. Through a great deal of prayer and God's provision, we paid off nearly the entire amount in three years. More importantly, there's not been a single day God hasn't provided for us since cutting up our credit cards.

There are a number of books and programs, but what it really takes to succeed is a heart for living as God intended us to live. How much more could we give if we had no debt? How much better would we sleep? How much easier would it be to hear God's voice without the deafening wall of debt between us and him?

WEEK FORTY-FIVE:
A Prayer for our Economy

H eir of all Things,[1] I have prayed for a renewal of fiscal stewardship in our nation and households. I pray now that the American economy would prosper as we obey your commands—it is you who gives us the ability to produce wealth.[2]

In The Word

[1] *Hebrews 1:2*

[2] *Deuteronomy 8:18*

[3] *Genesis 41:33-36*

May we turn back to your knowledge and seek the wisdom of your Word, for:

> *By wisdom a house is built,*
> *and through understanding it is*
> *established; through knowledge its rooms*
> *are filled with rare and beautiful treasures.*
> *(Proverbs 24:3-4)*

Like Joseph, let us plan for tomorrow instead of feasting on what is available today.[3] Help us to make wise decisions, reject debt, and grow our economy so the families of America will prosper.

Above all, may you be glorified by our actions. May we come to a place in our obedience where other nations are prompted to seek your blessing, and our prosperity is the banner of your favor.
AMEN.

"O powerful goodness! Bountiful Father! Merciful Guide! Increase in me that wisdom which discovers my truest interest. Strengthen my resolution to perform what that wisdom dictates. Accept my kind offices to thy other children as the only return in my power for thy continual favours to me."

-Benjamin Franklin

PATRIOT QUOTE

WEEK FORTY-SIX:
Prayer for the Homeless & Jobless

G od over all,[1] you have seen the suffering of America—those who are without work, those who have lost their homes and those who live in the streets. You have seen the brokenness of men struggling to provide for their families. You have heard the silent cries of mothers who cannot feed their children. You are close to the broken hearted and save the crushed spirit.[2]

In The Word

[1] *Romans 9:5*

[2] *Psalm 34:18*

[3] *Revelation 21:4*

[4] *Mark 12:31*

You have provided the answer to their plight in the church; you have blessed America with prosperity and wealth. Your Word commands us to deliver those who are in our reach:

> *If a brother or sister is without clothing and in need of daily food, and one of you says to them, "Go in peace, be warmed and be filled," and yet you do not give them what is necessary for their body, what use is that? (James 2:15-16)*

You have called us to do more than pray for those in need; you have commanded us to make a difference in their lives.

I pray for a change in my own heart and in the heart of the church. I pray for a revival in the soul of your people to see the jobless and

105

homeless of America through your eyes and with your compassion.

I pray for the encouragement and strength of those who are in need. Let them see your salvation through the apostles you send to deliver them. May we, as Christians, never view the government's generosity as an escape from our own responsibilities, but be grateful for the freedom it provides us to help one another.

Praise to our God who will bring a kingdom without pain or sorrow.[3] Until then, may we love and provide for our neighbor as you commanded us to do.[4] Allow the Christians of this nation to reflect your light through generosity and sacrifice.
   AMEN.

WEEK FORTY-SEVEN:

A Prayer for America's CEOs

ather God, I am grateful for the CEOs of America. Whether running a small business or a large corporation, they provide jobs and spur our economy. I pray, though, that we might never forget where true prosperity is born. You alone provide blessings,[1] and I pray our wealth will not blind us to the gospel.

In The Word

[1] *James 1:17*

[2] *Haggai 2:8*

[3] *1 Timothy 6:10*

All the gold and silver of our world belongs to you,[2] and you have commanded us to be stewards of your resources. May those who run American businesses love others more than profit and thereby receive the blessing of prosperity:

> *Command those who are rich in this present world not to be arrogant nor to put their hope in wealth, which is so uncertain, but to put their hope in God, who richly provides us with everything for our enjoyment. Command them to do good, to be rich in good deeds, and to be generous and willing to share. (1 Timothy 6:17-18)*

I pray for the continued success of our CEOs. Give prosperity and wealth to those who seek your will in the integrity of their business. Give encouragement to the small business owner, and protection to those who are tempted by a love of money over you. For wealth can be used to your glory, but the love of money is evil.[3]

Raise us up as a nation who gives you glory for our success, and bless the business owners who provide employment to the working families of America.

AMEN.

WEEK FORTY-EIGHT:
A Call to Physical Stewardship

C reator of all things,[1] you formed man in your likeness[2] so your name might be glorified. Then the very Word of God became flesh,[3] taking on the earthly body you created, so we might be saved.

You've not only called us to be stewards of the material resources you've given us, but of our physical bodies as well. Has our prosperity turned us from this responsibility? Forgive us our sin and change our hearts—for we have defiled your sanctuary:

> *Do you not know that your body is a temple of the Holy Spirit, who is in you, whom you have received from God? You are not your own; you were bought at a price. Therefore honor God with your body. (1 Corinthians 6:19-20)*

Do not let us be like Jeshurun, who abandoned its Creator.[4] Instead, let us present our bodies as living sacrifices,[5] so other nations will know we serve the Lord.

I pray for a call to physical stewardship in America, but also for you to reveal my own weaknesses. Teach me to honor your temple.
   AMEN.

In The Word

[1] *Colossians 1:16*

[2] *Genesis 1:27*

[3] *John 1:14*

[4] *Deu. 32:15*

[5] *Romans 12:1*

"The most eloquent prayer is the prayer through hands that heal and bless. The highest form of worship is the worship of unselfish Christian service. The greatest form of praise is the sound of consecrated feet seeking out the lost and helpless."

-Rev. Billy Graham

PATRIOT QUOTE

WEEK FORTY-NINE:
A Prayer for Healthcare Providers

H ealer of Nations,[1] you bring salvation to our soul and through your wounds we are healed.[2] I give praise to the Great Physician who has numbered the very hairs on my head.[3]

Thank you for the knowledge you've given us through science and medicine. All wisdom and knowledge comes through you.[4] I pray you would give discernment, wisdom and a steady hand to those whom you've anointed as healers.

Just as the Holy Spirit spoke through Luke, the beloved physician,[5] I pray our medical providers will see your hand in all things. For you are the source of our knowledge and healing:

> Praise the LORD, O my soul,
> and forget not all his benefits—
> who forgives all your sins
> and heals all your diseases.
> (Psalm 103:2-3)

I pray a blessing on our healthcare providers and ask for continued revelation in their fields of study. Thank you for the compassion and dedication you've placed within them.

In The Word

[1] *2 Chronicles 7:14*

[2] *Isaiah 53:5*

[3] *Matthew 10:30*

[4] *Proverbs 2:6*

[5] *Colossians 4:14*

[6] *Genesis 1:27*

You have given them a heart for helping others, which is a reflection of your love. I pray they might see the true source of that passion and give you praise.

What a wondrous gift to study your creation! The complexity of the human body is a testament to your greatness:

> *For you created my inmost being;*
> *you knit me together in my mother's womb.*
> *I praise you because I am fearfully and wonderfully made;*
> *your works are wonderful, I know that full well.*
> *(Psalm 139:13-14)*

Though you made us in your likeness,[6] our bodies became weak when sin entered the world. I know you have seen our suffering, and I'm grateful for the medical community you've given us. Give them the tools, knowledge and wisdom to heal our sick and cure our diseases. Above all, may we always acknowledge your hand in our salvation.
   AMEN.

WEEK FIFTY:

A Prayer for Widows and Orphans

God of the brokenhearted,[1] you have seen the devastation of hope in our land. How many children are without parents? How many parents are without spouses? You take notice when a single sparrow falls to the ground[2] and you care for those who are suffering.

You have called your children to meet the needs of those around them, but you have made a special plea for the care of widows and orphans:

> *Religion that God our Father accepts as pure and faultless is this: to look after orphans and widows in their distress and to keep oneself from being polluted by the world. (James 1:27)*

You are the father to the fatherless and the defender of widows.[3] Do not allow us to be like members of the early church, who ignored the very heart of your ministry! Instead, let us be like Stephen, who answered your call:[4]

Open my eyes to those in need around me. Direct me away from my own distractions and allow me to see people through your eyes.

Your wrath is stoked by the cries of the widows
and orphans who've been neglected.[5]
I pray for that same fire to be present in my heart.

I pray also that the church might have an outward focus on the
community, and for your name to be glorified through our actions.
May we truly be members of your body, doing your work with your
compassion and love.

    AMEN.

WEEK FIFTY-ONE:
A Prayer for America's Elderly

God of Wisdom and Ancient of Days,[1] your Word gives honor to the elderly and proclaims the value of their years. For wisdom is found among the aged, and long life brings understanding.[2]

You have commanded us to respect the elderly—to stand in deference when they enter a room.[3] For your word says:

> Gray hair is a crown of splendor;
> it is attained by a righteous life.
> (Proverbs 16:31)

Yet how many years of wisdom sit alone in rooms, neglected and dishonored? It breaks my heart to think of it.

Have we not honored our fathers and mothers?[3] Was this the first of your commandments to be neglected by our nation?[4] Has our unwillingness to heed their insight cost us our future? I pray it will not be so.

Give us, as a country, a heart for the elderly. Teach us to revere their teaching and honor their lives as you have commanded.
AMEN.

In The Word

[1] *Daniel 7:9*

[2] *Job 12:12*

[3] *Leviticus 19:32*

[4] *Exodus 20:12*

> "The cause of America is in a great measure the cause of all mankind. Where, say some, is the king of America? I'll tell you, friend, He reigns above."
>
> -Thomas Paine

WEEK FIFTY-TWO:
Our Coming King

L ion of the Tribe of Judah[1] and King of kings,[2] you answered the prayers of our founding fathers and made us a great nation! It was your hand that gave George Washington the gift of leadership and a hunger for freedom. You created Abraham Lincoln with a desire for equality and a heart for unification. You placed within Benjamin Franklin a longing to serve others as an act of worship. You led and strengthened us against all odds, and placed within these men a desire to serve you.

We are a great nation that serves a kingdom! Freedom and liberty can only be attained through your sovereign reign—for the foundation of your throne is righteousness and justice.[3]

Let us not forget your imminent return! All nations governed by men are fleeting, but you will establish an everlasting kingdom when you come again! You promised David his throne would last forever,[4] and Mary that her son would sit upon that throne for eternity.[5] May we not be forgotten when your throne is established on earth:[6]

In The Word

[1] *Revelation 5:5*

[2] *Revelation 19:16*

[3] *Psalm 89:14*

[4] *2 Samuel 7:11-16*

[5] *Luke 1:30-33*

[6] *Psalm 132:13-14*

[7] *Matthew 28:11-15*

Of the increase of his government and peace
there will be no end.
He will reign on David's throne
and over his kingdom,
establishing and upholding it
with justice and righteousness
from that time on and forever.
(Isaiah 9:7)

How will America be remembered in eternity?
Will its people bring to mind a nation of worship or rebellion?
Servants of their coming king or unfaithful stewards? Will we be a
people who welcome you or will we claim to be sleeping like the
Roman guards who denied your resurrection?[7]

I am so grateful that you blessed me with American citizenship!
Teach me, that I might never take my freedom for granted. I pray
that we, as a nation, would not squander our liberty on self
indulgence, but will constantly seek your will in our freedom. Teach
us to recapture the heart of Abraham Lincoln, who overheard a
soldier hoping you were on our side and replied:

> *"I am not at all concerned about that, for I know the Lord is*
> *always on the side of the right. But it is my constant anxiety and*
> *prayer that I and this nation should be on the Lord's side."*

May your name be glorified by the actions of the United States. May
the nations of the world look upon America and see a compassion,
generosity and prosperity that can only be explained by the touch of
your hand! May you keep this nation and its liberties safe until you
return and sit upon the throne of David. I ask these things in the
name of Jesus, the Lamb of our salvation and our coming King!
   AMEN.

PART THREE

Psalms for
Special Days of Prayer

A Prayer for New Year's Day

F ather of New Beginnings, your love and compassion is new every morning.[1] I come before you, standing at the threshold of a new year, with a dedicated and contrite heart.

Before I step into this new season, make clear to me anything I need to leave behind. Reveal my sin. Expose any unforgiving or negative thoughts in my heart so they might be left here—for you have said:

> "Forget the former things;
> do not dwell on the past.
> See, I am doing a new thing!
> Now it springs up; do you not perceive it?
> I am making a way in the desert
> and streams in the wasteland."
> (Isaiah 43:18-19)

Whatever trials I've been facing, I place them in your hands. Teach me, in this new year, to seek a closer relationship with you—for you have promised to draw near to those who seek you.[3]

During this year, I am dedicated to reading your Word, listening for your direction, praying and fasting. I also commit myself to praying for America and for those in authority over me.[2]

In The Word

[1] *Lam. 3:22-23*

[2] *2 Timothy 2:1-3*

[3] *James 4:8*

[4] *Isaiah 46:10*

Only you know the end from the beginning,[4] and I trust in your sovereignty. You know exactly what our nation will face this year, and I ask the Holy Spirit to reveal what I should be praying for.

Give me a heart for the president and his family, even when I disagree with him. Erase any prejudice of partisanship from within me so I might pray for your will over my own. Teach me how to serve my community and country by serving the Kingdom, and allow me to encourage other Christians to pray for our nation.

I ask for your blessing on America this year. May you be given glory for our prosperity, and may we seek you in times of trouble.
    AMEN.

A Prayer for Easter

God of Firstfruits,[1] you brought us freedom through your sacrifice. Praise be to the God of Creation[2] who sacrificed his only son to redeem those who believe in him![3]

Our freedom does not come from the institution of government; it is not granted by the Constitution or Bill of Rights. Irrevocable freedom comes only through your grace:

> *Now the Lord is the Spirit, and where the Spirit of the Lord is, there is freedom. (2 Corinthians 3:17)*

I pray, this Easter Sunday, for those who serve our country—whether dining at the White House, returning home from Washington, or deployed around the world, I ask for a blessing on their households.

On this day, we celebrate your mercy toward us. May we be reminded of your great sacrifice and compassion. If you gave your only child for us while we were still sinners, how much more will you do for those who belong to you?[4]
Help us, in this season, to remain focused on you. Teach us to hear your voice so we might serve you in response to our salvation.
  AMEN.

In The Word

[1] *1 Cor. 15:20-23*

[2] *Genesis 1:1*

[3] *John 3:16*

[4] *Romans 5:8-9*

"And now, Almighty Father, if it is Thy holy will that we shall obtain a place and name among the nations of the earth, grant that we may be enabled to show our gratitude for Thy goodness by our endeavors to fear and obey Thee."

-George Washington

PATRIOT QUOTE

The National Day of Prayer

F ather God, you are great and worthy of praise.[1] I am grateful for the mercy you have conferred on the United States. You have promised to heal our land if we humble ourselves before you,[2] and today we do so in a special day of prayer.

I am dedicated to praying for my country, but today is different. America itself has petitioned its people for prayer on this day—we do not pray as individuals, but as one unified nation under God. You are the source of our prosperity and Christ is the hope of our future:

> *"Here is my servant whom I have chosen,*
> *the one I love, in whom I delight;*
> *I will put my Spirit on him,*
> *and he will proclaim justice to the nations...*
> *In his name the nations will put their*
> *hope." (Matthew 12:18, 21)*

I join with the president in asking for your guidance, mercy and protection on our country. I thank you for the liberty and freedom you have bestowed on the United States and give you praise!

I lift up my president and his staff to you. May the Holy Spirit give them both the gift of

In The Word

[1] *Psalm 145:3*

[2] *2 Chronicles 7:14*

[3] *Romans 12:5-8*

[4] *1 Timothy 2:1-2*

leadership and servitude.[3] I do not know the struggles they face, but I pray for them to be encouraged and strengthened through a relationship with you.

I ask your blessing on American troops serving away from their loved ones, and for your comforting hand to be on the families awaiting their safe return.

I pray for the sovereignty of America. Give us the strength to stand with our allies, but the will to stand alone when necessary. Through seeking your will, may our sovereignty be a light to other nations and a hope to those in need.

Above all, teach us to be a nation dedicated to your Word. Teach us to pray for our leaders[4] and seek your face. May we not be a Christian nation by mere proclamation, but through our actions, mercy and compassion.

   AMEN.

A Prayer for Memorial Day

C omforter and Councilor,[1] We turn to you in our time of grief; our help comes from the Lord, maker of heaven and earth.[2] Since the Civil War, we have set aside a day for remembrance, and our hearts are broken for the men and women who have been lost while serving our country.

In The Word

[1] *John 14:26*

[2] *Psalm 121:3*

[3] *1 Corinthians 6:20*

[4] *Hebrews 4:15*

[5] *Psalm 56:8*

Neither national liberty nor eternal freedom comes without a price. You paid for our eternal salvation with your own son,[3] and you feel the suffering[4] of parents who've lost their children defending America's freedom. You have heard the cries of spouses, children, siblings and friends. You have collected their tears[5] and will be their comfort:

> *Praise be to the God and Father of our Lord Jesus Christ, the Father of compassion and the God of all comfort, who comforts us in all our troubles, so that we can comfort those in any trouble with the comfort we ourselves have received from God.*
> *(2 Corinthians 1:3-4)*

I am grateful for those who have died defending my freedom. Do not allow me to become complacent toward their sacrifice, but exercise my freedom to benefit my country and your

Kingdom. Remind me daily that my freedom in both life and eternity came at a price someone else paid.

For hundreds of years, men and women have sacrificed themselves for my right to pursue happiness. They have shown the true meaning of love, for:

> *Greater love has no one than this, that he lay down his life for his friends. (John 15:13)*

I am grateful to those individuals, and my heart turns toward the family members who are left behind. This day is a reminder of their sacrifice and I pray the Holy Spirit would comfort them.
AMEN.

A Prayer for Independence Day

Mighty God,[1] you are to be desired by all nations,[2] yet chose to make America great. With celebration for our nation's birth, I come before you with thanksgiving for the freedom bestowed on me each day anew. Praise be to the Lord who granted and preserves our independence!

From our earliest days, you have made us a nation of strength and compassion because we sought your favor. John Adams was right when he wrote of Independence Day, saying:

> *"It ought to be commemorated, as the day of deliverance, by solemn acts of devotion to God Almighty."*

Have we forgotten that you are our deliverer, refuge and fortress?[3] It is you alone, our Creator, who endows us with the right to the life, liberty and pursuit of happiness our Declaration of Independence speaks of. True freedom is not granted by a piece of paper, but through the sacrifice of Jesus, our savior:

> *It is for freedom that Christ has set us free. Stand firm, then, and do not let yourselves be burdened again by a yoke of slavery. (Galatians 5:1)*

In The Word

[1] *Isaiah 9:6*

[2] *Haggai 2:7*

[3] *Psalm 18:2*

[4] *Psalm 19:1-4*

129

Let us be forever watchful of our hearts, that we may not blindly fall into the slavery of sin and pride. Instead, let the skies above our land be a reminder of your hand in creation.[4] Let their beauty direct us, with thankful spirits, toward your will in America. Let us embrace the words spoken by Samuel Adams as the Declaration of Independence was being signed:

> *"We have this day restored the Sovereign to Whom all men ought to be obedient. He reigns in heaven and from the rising to the setting of the sun, let His kingdom come."*

On this Independence Day, we do not celebrate our own accomplishments, but yours through us. May you receive the glory for America's greatness, and may we be faithful stewards of your gospel to the nations.

    AMEN.

A Prayer for September Eleventh

F ather God, you are our strength in times of trouble.[1] Today we are reminded of a wound in our nation's history. We are grateful for the soldiers, fire fighters and police officers who voluntarily placed themselves in harm's way to protect us—so many of our brave first responders were lost. This day is also filled with the remembrance of innocent victims who've lost their lives.

We know you are a God who sees our pain and comes close to the brokenhearted.[2] Unlike many of our nation's solemn days, we still remember the twisted metal and smoke rising into the horizon over New York, the Pentagon and Pennsylvania. For many, it is still a day of loss and suffering.

We remember the fear and uncertainty we felt that September morning. But like the Americans at Fort McHenry in 1814, we also remember the hope you gave us as the smoke began to clear and we saw our star-spangled banner, still waving, unfurled over the battlefield our enemies meant to be our place of defeat. Lord, encourage and strengthen us on this day.

In The Word

[1] *Psalm 46:1*

[2] *Psalm 34:18*

[3] *2 Cor. 1:3-4*

[4] *John 14:16*

I confess there are some of us who are still angry—some still live in fear. Send the Holy Spirit to comfort us, and give us the strength to comfort one another.[3] Remind us that we have victory in Christ, and that we can find rest in you:

> *When you lie down, you will not be afraid;*
> *when you lie down, your sleep will be sweet.*
> *Have no fear of sudden disaster*
> *or of the ruin that overtakes the wicked,*
> *for the LORD will be your confidence*
> *and will keep your foot from being snared.*
> *(Proverbs 3:24-26)*

I pray a blessing of peace on the families who mourn the loss of their loved ones—whether a flight passenger, office worker, fire fighter, police officer or member of the military, each one of the people lost that morning had friends and families who suffer in silence today. May the Comforter[4] be sent to their side, and may our communities rise up to meet their needs. Protect our hearts and strengthen our resolve.

    AMEN.

A Prayer for Election Season

Sovereign Lord,[1] I come before you as our nation prepares to elect new leaders. Our hearts make our plans, but you direct our path.[2] There is no government on earth you did not allow[3]—I pray, then, that we would be in your will as we choose our leaders.

In The Word

[1] *Jeremiah 32:17*

[2] *Psalm 16:9*

[3] *Romans 13:1*

[4] *Psalm 25:21*

[5] *James 3:3-12*

Between the pundits, talking points and negative advertisements, it's easy to become cynical about our election process, but remind me of the great freedom I've been given in that process. May I not take for granted my right to speak directly into our country's governance.

I also lift up the men and women who are running for office. It is a grueling process for the candidates and their families. May they seek you and have your protection through the integrity and honesty of their campaigns:[4]

> *For the LORD grants wisdom!*
> *From his mouth come knowledge and*
> *understanding. He grants a treasure of*
> *common sense to the honest.*
> *He is a shield to those who walk with*
> *integrity. He guards the paths of the just*
> *and protects those who are faithful to him.*
> *(Psalm 2:6-8, NLT)*

Direct my actions and guard my tongue[5] in this election season as I trust in your promise:

> *I will instruct you and teach you in the way you should go;*
> *I will counsel you and watch over you. (Psalm 32:8)*

Do not allow me to be swayed by partisanship or to become slothful in vetting our candidates. Reveal any ungodly bias in my heart before I cast my vote, and teach me to seek your wisdom over my own.

May your will be done in this election, and may I be an instrument of your desire.
AMEN.

A Prayer for Veterans Day

Prince of Peace,[1] you see those who are burdened by the emotional and physical scars of war. We are grateful for the soldiers who've sacrificed their lives defending freedom, but let us not forget the men and women who live among us as veterans.

You have commanded us to honor those who came before us:

> *Remember the days of old; consider the generations long past. Ask your father and he will tell you, your elders, and they will explain to you. (Deuteronomy 32:7)*

Yet there are many veterans whose stories have not been told. There are soldiers of sacrifice who suffer in silence with bodies no longer responding to their command. There are veterans plagued by the chaos of trauma and nightmares, but you have formed their hearts and seen them.[2]

Deliver these men and women from their trials, for you are not a God of disorder, but of peace.[3] Send the Holy Spirit to comfort and draw them toward you. For you have promised to carry our burdens:

> *"Come to me, all you who are weary and burdened, and I will give you rest. Take my yoke upon you and learn from me, for I am gentle and humble in heart, and you will find rest for your souls. For my yoke is easy and my burden is light."*
> *(Matthew 11:28-30)*

May the households of our veterans be blessed today, and may our nation recognize the importance and severity of their sacrifice. May their lives be honored and their history remembered.

I am grateful for the soldiers who serve away from their families so I might live in liberty with mine. Bless them with prosperity and peace.

    AMEN.

A Prayer for Thanksgiving Day

B read of Life,[1] you are the provider of all good things. Praise be to the God of grace on this day of Thanksgiving! You meet our needs with abundance so we might share with others.[2] You instituted many feasts for your people, and as we feast in celebration today, do not let us forget that man does not live by bread only, but through your Word:[3]

In The Word

[1] *John 6:35*

[2] *2 Corinthians 9:8*

[3] *Matthew 4:4*

> *Come, let us sing for joy to the LORD;*
> *let us shout aloud to the Rock of our*
> *salvation.*
> *Let us come before him with thanksgiving*
> *and extol him with music and song.*
> *(Psalm 95:1-2)*

You have bestowed strength, power and wealth upon our nation. You have granted us such bounty that I'm fearful we take our prosperity for granted. Let us be reminded on this day of your grace in our lives.

I am grateful for my family and my liberty; I thank you for the friends in my life that grant joy; I praise you for a nation that recognizes my right to give you thanksgiving. May our leaders be blessed and may our country find your favor.
    AMEN.

> *"The rights of man come not from the generosity of the state but from the hand of God."*
>
> -John F. Kennedy

PATRIOT QUOTE

Pearl Harbor Remembrance Day

L ight of the World,[1] you are the hope of our
nation's future and we seek your light in the
dark memory of our mourning. Today we
remember the largest military strike on
American soil with sorrow for the lost and
gratitude for your deliverance.

The U.S.S. Arizona Memorial in Hawaii serves
as the final resting place for over one thousand
American soldiers and as a reminder of those
who would be lost in World War II. The United
States was led into war against the very enemies
of God who sought the destruction of your
people:

> *For our struggle is not against flesh and*
> *blood, but against the rulers, against the*
> *authorities, against the powers of this dark*
> *world and against the spiritual forces of*
> *evil in the heavenly realms.*
> *(Ephesians 6:12)*

I'm grateful America was used as an instrument
of liberation for the oppressed and for the
protection of your chosen people.[2] We mourn,
however, for the lives that were lost and seek
your grace. May we have your continued favor
as we safeguard the children of Abraham.[3]

In The Word

[1] *John 8:12*

[2] *Deu. 14:2*

[3] *Genesis 12:3*

[4] *Deu. 32:7*

[5] *Ephesians 6:13-18*

You have commanded us to remember the days of old and seek the stories of our elders.[4] I pray the memories and stories of our veterans would not be forgotten today.

Give us a heart for the American soldier and reverence for those who have passed. Millions of free men and women throughout the globe owe a debt of gratitude to the Allied soldiers of that war.

Today we remember those who were lost in that first attack on Pearl Harbor and ask your hand of protection to be upon us. May our leaders seek your wisdom and our people don your armor[5] that we might have you as our shield.

    AMEN.

A Prayer for Christmas Day

I mmanuel,[1] you are our Wonderful Councilor and Prince of Peace.[2] Today we celebrate the birth of true freedom, which is in Christ. If you had not stepped into our world as a child, we would never have known the freedom and liberty of salvation—the ideals of our founding fathers never would have been formed.

We thank you for our nation, but recognize that you didn't come into the world for America, but for all mankind; you came that we might see a day without war and without borders. You came, born in a manger, so we might be reunited with an Everlasting Father who stepped out of eternity[3] to save his children:

> *And there were shepherds living out in the fields nearby, keeping watch over their flocks at night. An angel of the Lord appeared to them, and the glory of the Lord shone around them, and they were terrified. But the angel said to them, "Do not be afraid. I bring you good news of great joy that will be for all the people. Today in the town of David a Savior has been born to you; he is Christ the Lord."*
> *(Luke 2:8-11)*

Mighty God, thank you for sending your son to redeem us. You have seen the pain of this world

In The Word

[1] *Matthew 1:23*

[2] *Isaiah 9:6*

[3] *John 1:1-5, 14*

[4] *John 14:16*

[5] *Romans 13:1*

141

and sent us an advocate and comforter.[4]

I pray for the leaders of our nation. In this Christmas season, may their households be blessed for their service, and may they be reminded of your grace in establishing their posts.[5] May they seek your favor in the coming year and be granted the gift of wisdom.

Above all, I lift up the men and women of our armed forces who cannot be with their families this Christmas. Protect our soldiers and comfort their loved ones. Remind us of their sacrifice as we worship your plan of salvation, singing with the heavenly hosts:

> *Glory to God in the highest, and on earth peace,*
> *good will toward men. (Luke 2:14, KJV)*
>
> *AMEN.*

A Prayer During Natural Disasters

M aker of heaven and earth, the sea and everything in them,[1] we worship the God who is faithful! We live in a broken world, and creation itself groans, as if in childbirth, awaiting your return.[2]

Our nation is facing a terrible catastrophe, and we turn to you for comfort and guidance:

> *God is our refuge and strength, an ever-present help in trouble. Therefore we will not fear, though the earth give way and the mountains fall into the heart of the sea, though its waters roar and foam and the mountains quake with their surging. Selah. (Psalm 46:1-3)*

You are a God who sees us,[3] and we know you feel our suffering. Our hearts are broken for those who have lost loved ones, and there may be many who do not yet know if their families are safe. I ask you to send the Holy Spirit to comfort them.

For those who have lost their homes, give them provision. For those who are trapped, awaiting rescue, give them hope.

I pray a blessing on the rescue workers

In The Word

[1] *Psalm 146:6*

[2] *Romans 8:22*

[3] *Genesis 16:13*

[4] *Psalm 119:105*

[5] *1 Cor. 12:12-14*

responding to this natural disaster. Be a lamp unto their feet[4] and guide their steps. Strengthen their senses and grant them the gift of discernment.

I pray for the delivery of food and water to those who are in need. Bring medical supplies, housing and transportation to those who have been affected by this tragedy. Let our hope be in your promise:

> *"Though the mountains be shaken*
> *and the hills be removed,*
> *yet my unfailing love for you will not be shaken*
> *nor my covenant of peace be removed,"*
> *says the LORD, who has compassion on you.*
> *(Isaiah 54:10)*

Above all, mobilize the body of Christ[5] to do you work; reveal what you would have each of us do in this crisis. May we not be passive observers, but instruments of your compassion to those in need.
   AMEN.

PART FOUR

Praying Patriot Worksheets

Real Prayers for Real People

he Praying Patriot Worksheets are designed to help you focus
your prayers for the nation. Remember, scripture tells us to pray
for those individuals in authority over us, not their positions (I
Timothy 2:1-3). It's easy to say a generic prayer for the office of the
presidency, but it's impersonal. Would you pray for one of your best
friends facing adversity by saying, "Dear Lord, I lift up the position of
my second best friend to you?" Of course not. So why would we
generalize prayers for those who are leading our nation?

When Abram and Sarai were commissioned by God, he changed their
names to Abraham and Sarah; Jacob became Israel, Jesus changed
Simon's name to Peter and Saul became Paul. When God looks at me
he doesn't see my job title; he sees Joshua. When he looks at
President Bush or President Obama he doesn't see their office, but
the children he created to serve in that office. When God listens to
your prayers, he embraces them with your name on his heart. Names
are important to God and they should be important to us.

You may say, "That's a lot of names to remember, and God knows
who they are," but prayer isn't about informing God, it's about letting
him inform us. Yes, God knows their names, but when you really
start praying for people by name, it will change *your* heart. The most
difficult aspect of praying for our national leadership is that we often
disagree with them—this is why it's so important to personalize our
prayers.

Whether praying for the president, your local representative, or your child's teacher, be sure to use their name. Remember their families and focus on how God sees them rather than whether or not you agree with them.

Use the Praying Patriot Worksheets as a reminder to pray for those in authority as individuals—remembering they have their own trials, families and spiritual walk. Ask God to reveal how he wants you to pray for them, and to change your heart toward our leaders when necessary. Remember the prayers for our nation are more about your relationship with our sovereign King than its earthly leaders.

Praying for the Presidency

I urge, then, first of all, that requests, prayers, intercession and thanksgiving be made for everyone—for kings and all those in authority...
(1 Timothy 2:1-2)

FAMILY

PRESIDENT:
_____

PRESIDENT'S SPOUSE:
_____

PRESIDENT'S CHILDREN:
_____
_____
_____

LIVING PARENTS:
_____
_____

STAFF

CHIEF OF STAFF:
_____

DEPUTY CHIEFS OF STAFF:
_____
_____

SENIOR ADVISORS:
_____
_____

COUNSELOR:
_____

PRAYER REMINDERS

☐ Is the president visiting foreign soil for any reason?

☐ What are the most difficult issues facing the president?

☐ Does the president have any major speeches or events coming up?

☐ What legislation is about to make its way to the president's desk?

☐ Have I asked God to reveal how I should be praying for my president?

_____
_____
_____
_____
_____
_____
_____
_____
_____
_____
_____
_____
_____
_____
_____

PRAYER NOTES

Write down how you feel the Holy Spirit is prompting you to pray for your president. Be sure to spend time asking God to reveal his will in your prayer life.

_____

_____

_____

_____

_____

_____

_____

_____

_____

_____

_____

_____

BIBLE VERSES

As you read the Bible, ask God to inspire your prayer life through his Word. Write down the verses that stick out to you, even if you're not sure how to use them yet.

_____

_____

_____

_____

_____

_____

_____

_____

_____

_____

_____

_____

Be sure to come back to this worksheet or review your prayer journal in the future. See how God has answered your prayers and used his Word to transform you.

Praying for the President's Cabinet

I urge, then, first of all, that requests, prayers, intercession and thanksgiving be made for everyone—for kings and all those in authority...
(1 Timothy 2:1-2)

CABINET MEMBERS

VICE PRESIDENT:
_____

ATTORNEY GENERAL:
_____

SECRETARY OF STATE:
_____

SEC. OF DEFENSE:
_____

SEC. OF THE TREASURY:
_____

SEC. OF THE INTERIOR:
_____

SEC. OF AGRICULTURE:
_____

SEC. OF COMMERCE:
_____

SEC. OF LABOR:
_____

SEC. OF ENERGY:
_____

SEC. OF HEALTH AND
HUMAN SERVICES:
_____

SEC. OF VETERANS AFFAIRS:
_____

SEC. OF EDUCATION:
_____

SEC. OF TRANSPORTATION:
_____

SEC. OF HOUSING AND
URBAN DEVELOPMENT:
_____

SEC. OF HOMELAND
SECURITY:
_____

PRAYER REMINDERS

_____
_____
_____
_____
_____
_____
_____
_____
_____
_____
_____
_____
_____
_____

PRAYER NOTES

Write down how you feel the Holy Spirit is prompting you to pray for the President's Cabinet. Spend time asking God to reveal his will in your prayer life.

_____

_____

_____

_____

_____

_____

_____

_____

_____

_____

_____

_____

_____

BIBLE VERSES

As you read the Bible, ask God to inspire your prayer life through his Word. Write down the verses that stick out to you, even if you're not sure how to use them yet.

_____

_____

_____

_____

_____

_____

_____

_____

_____

_____

_____

Be sure to come back to this worksheet or review your prayer journal in the future. See how God has answered your prayers and used his Word to transform you.

Praying for First Responders

FIRE DEPARTMENT

CHIEF:

_____

FIRE FIGHTER NAME, RANK:

_____

FIRE FIGHTER NAME, RANK:

_____

FIRE FIGHTER NAME, RANK:

_____

FIRE FIGHTER NAME, RANK:

_____

FIRE FIGHTER NAME, RANK:

_____

EMS

NAME:

_____

NAME:

_____

NAME:

_____

NAME:

_____

LAW ENFORCEMENT

CHIEF:

_____

POLICE OFFICER NAME, RANK:

_____

POLICE OFFICER NAME, RANK:

_____

POLICE OFFICER NAME, RANK:

_____

POLICE OFFICER NAME, RANK:

_____

EMERGENCY NUMBERS

_____
_____
_____
_____
_____
_____
_____
_____
_____
_____
_____
_____

PRAYER NOTES

Write down how you feel the Holy Spirit is prompting you to pray for first responders in your town. Spend time asking God to reveal his will in your prayer

_____

_____

_____

_____

_____

_____

_____

_____

_____

_____

_____

_____

_____

BIBLE VERSES

As you read the Bible, ask God to inspire your prayer life through his Word. Write down the verses that stick out to you, even if you're not sure how to use them yet.

_____

_____

_____

_____

_____

_____

_____

_____

_____

_____

_____

_____

Be sure to come back to this worksheet or review your prayer journal in the future. See how God has answered your prayers and used his Word to transform you.

Praying for the Local Military

*I urge, then, first of all, that requests, prayers, intercession and thanksgiving
be made for everyone—for kings and all those in authority...*
(1 Timothy 2:1-2)

STATE NATIONAL GUARD

ADJUTANT GENERAL:

_____

CHAPLAIN:

_____

SOLDIER NAME, RANK:

_____

SOLDIER NAME, RANK:

_____

SOLDIER NAME, RANK:

_____

SOLDIER NAME, RANK:

_____

SOLDIER NAME, RANK:

_____

SOLDIER NAME, RANK:

_____

SOLDIER NAME, RANK:

_____

SOLDIER NAME, RANK:

_____

LOCAL TROOPS WHO ARE DEPLOYED

NAME	RANK	BRANCH	NOTES
FAMILY:			

NAME	RANK	BRANCH	NOTES
FAMILY:			

NAME	RANK	BRANCH	NOTES
FAMILY:			

_____

_____

_____

LOCAL TROOPS WHO ARE DEPLOYED

NAME   RANK   BRANCH   NOTES

FAMILY:_____

NAME   RANK   BRANCH   NOTES

FAMILY:_____

NAME   RANK   BRANCH   NOTES

FAMILY:_____

NAME   RANK   BRANCH   NOTES

FAMILY:_____

PRAYER NOTES

Write down how you feel the Holy Spirit is prompting you to pray for your local soldiers. Spend time asking God to reveal his will in your prayer life.

Praying for State Government

I urge, then, first of all, that requests, prayers, intercession and thanksgiving be made for everyone—for kings and all those in authority...
(1 Timothy 2:1-2)

GOVERNOR

GOVERNOR:

_____

GOVERNOR'S SPOUSE:

_____

GOVERNOR'S CHILDREN:

_____

_____

_____

OFFICIALS

LIEUTENANT GOVERNOR:

_____

SECRETARY OF STATE:

_____

ATTORNEY GENERAL:

_____

TREASURER:

_____

AUDITOR:

_____

OTHER:

_____

U.S. CONGRESS

SENATORS:

_____

_____

REPRESENTATIVES:

_____

_____

_____

_____

_____

_____

_____

_____

_____

LOCAL REPRESENTATIVES

_____

_____

_____

_____

_____

_____

_____

_____

_____

PRAYER NOTES

Write down how you feel the Holy Spirit is prompting you to pray for your state officials. Spend time asking God to reveal his will in your prayer life.

_____

_____

_____

_____

_____

_____

_____

_____

_____

_____

_____

_____

BIBLE VERSES

As you read the Bible, ask God to inspire your prayer life through his Word. Write down the verses that stick out to you, even if you're not sure how to use them yet.

_____

_____

_____

_____

_____

_____

_____

_____

_____

_____

_____

_____

_____

Be sure to come back to this worksheet or review your prayer journal in the future. See how God has answered your prayers and used his Word to transform you.

Praying for Town Government

I urge, then, first of all, that requests, prayers, intercession and thanksgiving be made for everyone—for kings and all those in authority...
(1 Timothy 2:1-2)

TOWN OFFICIALS

MAYOR:

_____

TOWN MANAGER:

_____

TOWN CLERK:

_____

PUBLIC WORKS:

_____

ASSESSOR:

_____

TREASURER:

_____

PARKS & RECREATION:

_____

LIBRARY:

_____

CHIEF OF POLICE:

_____

FIRE CHIEF:

_____

OTHER:

_____
_____

SELECT BOARD

MEMBERS:

_____
_____
_____
_____
_____
_____
_____
_____
_____
_____
_____
_____

PRAYER REMINDERS

_____
_____
_____
_____
_____
_____
_____
_____
_____
_____
_____
_____
_____

PRAYER NOTES

Write down how you feel the Holy Spirit is prompting you to pray for your town officials. Spend time asking God to reveal his will in your prayer life.

_____

_____

_____

_____

_____

_____

_____

_____

_____

_____

_____

_____

BIBLE VERSES

As you read the Bible, ask God to inspire your prayer life through his Word. Write down the verses that stick out to you, even if you're not sure how to use them yet.

_____

_____

_____

_____

_____

_____

_____

_____

_____

_____

_____

Be sure to come back to this worksheet or review your prayer journal in the future. See how God has answered your prayers and used his Word to transform you.

Praying for the Local School

SCHOOL OFFICIALS

SUPERINTENDENT:

_____

PRINCIPAL:

_____

VICE PRINCIPAL:

_____

COUNSELOR:

_____

NURSE:

_____

SCHOOL BOARD

MEMBERS:

_____

_____

_____

_____

_____

_____

_____

_____

_____

EDUCATORS

NAME: SUBJECT: PRAYER REMINDER:

_____

_____

_____

_____

_____

_____

_____

_____

_____

_____

_____

PRAYER NOTES

Write down how you feel the Holy Spirit is prompting you to pray for your local school. Spend time asking God to reveal his will in your prayer life.

_____

_____

_____

_____

_____

_____

_____

_____

_____

_____

_____

BIBLE VERSES

As you read the Bible, ask God to inspire your prayer life through his Word. Write down the verses that stick out to you, even if you're not sure how to use them yet.

_____

_____

_____

_____

_____

_____

_____

_____

_____

_____

_____

_____

Be sure to come back to this worksheet or review your prayer journal in the future. See how God has answered your prayers and used his Word to transform you.

My Personal Prayer List

REMEMBER TO PRAY FOR:

NAME:
_____

NOTES:_____
_____
_____

NAME:
_____

NOTES:_____
_____
_____

NAME:
_____

NOTES:_____
_____
_____

NAME:
_____

NOTES:_____
_____
_____
_____
_____
_____
_____

NAME:
_____

NOTES:_____
_____
_____

NAME:
_____

NOTES:_____
_____
_____

PRAYER REMINDERS

- ☐ _____
- ☐ _____
- ☐ _____
- ☐ _____
- ☐ _____
- ☐ _____
- ☐ _____
- ☐ _____
- ☐ _____
- ☐ _____
- ☐ _____
- ☐ _____
- ☐ _____

PRAYER NOTES

Write down how you feel the Holy Spirit is prompting you to pray. Spend time asking God to reveal his will in your prayer life.

_____

_____

_____

_____

_____

_____

_____

_____

_____

_____

_____

_____

_____

_____

BIBLE VERSES

As you read the Bible, ask God to inspire your prayer life through his Word. Write down the verses that stick out to you, even if you're not sure how to use them yet.

_____

_____

_____

_____

_____

_____

_____

_____

_____

_____

_____

_____

Be sure to come back to this worksheet or review your prayer journal in the future. See how God has answered your prayers and used his Word to transform you.

My Personal Prayer List

I urge, then, first of all, that requests, prayers, intercession and thanksgiving be made for everyone—for kings and all those in authority...
(1 Timothy 2:1-2)

REMEMBER TO PRAY FOR:

NAME:
_____

NOTES:_____
_____
_____

NAME:
_____

NOTES:_____
_____
_____

NAME:
_____

NOTES:_____
_____
_____

NAME:
_____

NOTES:_____
_____
_____
_____
_____
_____
_____

NAME:
_____

NOTES:_____
_____
_____

NAME:
_____

NOTES:_____
_____
_____

PRAYER REMINDERS

- ☐ _____
- ☐ _____
- ☐ _____
- ☐ _____
- ☐ _____
- ☐ _____
- ☐ _____
- ☐ _____
- ☐ _____
- ☐ _____
- ☐ _____
- ☐ _____
- ☐ _____

Index of Patriot Quotes

*Quotations sourced from *America's God and Country Encyclopedia of Quotations* by William J. Federer and are used by permission of the author.

Index of Bible References

Notes

Notes

Notes

MINI PAUL REVERE — Joshua Masters of Milan charges on an immovable horse and holds a well-lit lantern in celebration of America's 200th birthday during the "Happy Birthday America" parade in Milan Saturday.

Joshua's love of country started early in life. He's shown here as the blue-ribbon winner in a bicentennial parade. The Berlin (NH) Reporter—June 10, 1976. Reprinted with permission.

About the Author

Joshua J. Masters is a pastor, author and Christian speaker. He was first accredited by the Christian and Missionary Alliance and has served in multiple areas of ministry. As a member of the Screen Actors Guild (SAG-AFTRA), he's also comfortable working both in front of and behind the camera. He is passionate about ministries that reach out to hurting people while growing new believers into leaders. His work has a focus on spiritual formation, care and outreach. Joshua lives with his wife, Gina and their dog, Franklin.

Learn more at:
www.joshuajmasters.com

www.ingramcontent.com/pod-product-compliance
Lightning Source LLC
Chambersburg PA
CBHW021926040426
42448CB00008B/938